A dream is a wish your heart makes, when you're fast asleep.

SHABBY & BEYOND
SCRAPBOOKING IDEAS

A TweetyJill Publication

ACKNOWLEDGEMENTS

Copyright by TweetyJill Publications 2006 • Shabby & Beyond Scrapbooking Ideas

Published and created by TweetyJill Publications • 5824 Bee Ridge Road, PMB 412 • Sarasota, FL 34233

For information about wholesale, please contact customer service at www.tweetyjill.com or 1-800-595-5497

Printed in China • ISBN 1-891898-09-4

Artists: Kim Henkel, Lesley Riley, Jill Haglund, Roben-Marie Smith, Amy Wellenstein, Nikki Cleary,
Carolyn Peeler, Karen Hamad, M.D. and Carlene Federer

Book Design: Laurie Doherty • Book Layout: Jill Haglund
Editor: Lisa Codianne Fowler • Assistant Editor: Donna Marie Marcantonio

Photography: Herb Booth of Herb Booth Studios, Inc., Sarasota, FL

TABLE OF CONTENTS

SHABBY & BEYOND SCRAPBOOKING IDEAS WAS CONCEIVED WITH YOU IN MIND.

*A*s you read through these pages you will be mesmerized by the eclectic scrapbook layouts designed by some of the most creative artists in the industry: Kim Henkel, Lesley Riley, Jill Haglund, Carlene Federer, Roben-Marie Smith, Amy Wellenstein, Carolyn Peeler, Nikki Cleary and Karen Hamad, M.D.

We specifically chose them to inspire you with ideas because they enjoy creating with the same materials you do! They love scrapbooking, card-making, stamping and quilting, along with all paper, photo and fabric arts! Wouldn't you agree that pretty much covers all the bases for being on the cutting edge of crafts today?

Most of the artists travel extensively, teach nationally, and have been featured in numerous popular scrapbooking, quilting and paper crafts publications. You can learn more about each artist by reading their individual biographies at the beginning of each artist's chapter.

You will enjoy discovering, as you delve into the materials list, that these talented ladies not only frequent craft stores,

but also scour antique shops, garage sales and flea markets for the perfect embellishments to achieve that finishing touch. We all know how much fun that can be, and now we know we are not alone — the best of the best do it too, for some small but thrilling authentic find to layer onto a page!

We feel privileged to be able to feature the breath-taking work of so many women, and know you will savor the detailed close-ups of their artistry.

So pour yourself a cup of tea, curl up in your favorite chair and get ready for a visual treat!

Jill Haglund
Founder and President

TweetyJill Publications:
- *The Complete Guide to Scrapbooking*
- *The Idea Book to Scrapbooking*
- *Scrapbooking for Kids (Ages 1-100)*
- *Scrapbooking as a Learning Tool*
- *Artists Creating with Photos*
- *Creating Vintage Cards*
- *Making Cards with Rubber Stamps, Ribbons & Buttons*
- *Shabby & Beyond Scrapbooking Ideas*
- *Rubber Stamped Artists Trading Cards (ATCs)*
- *Great Gifts using Scrapbooking Materials*

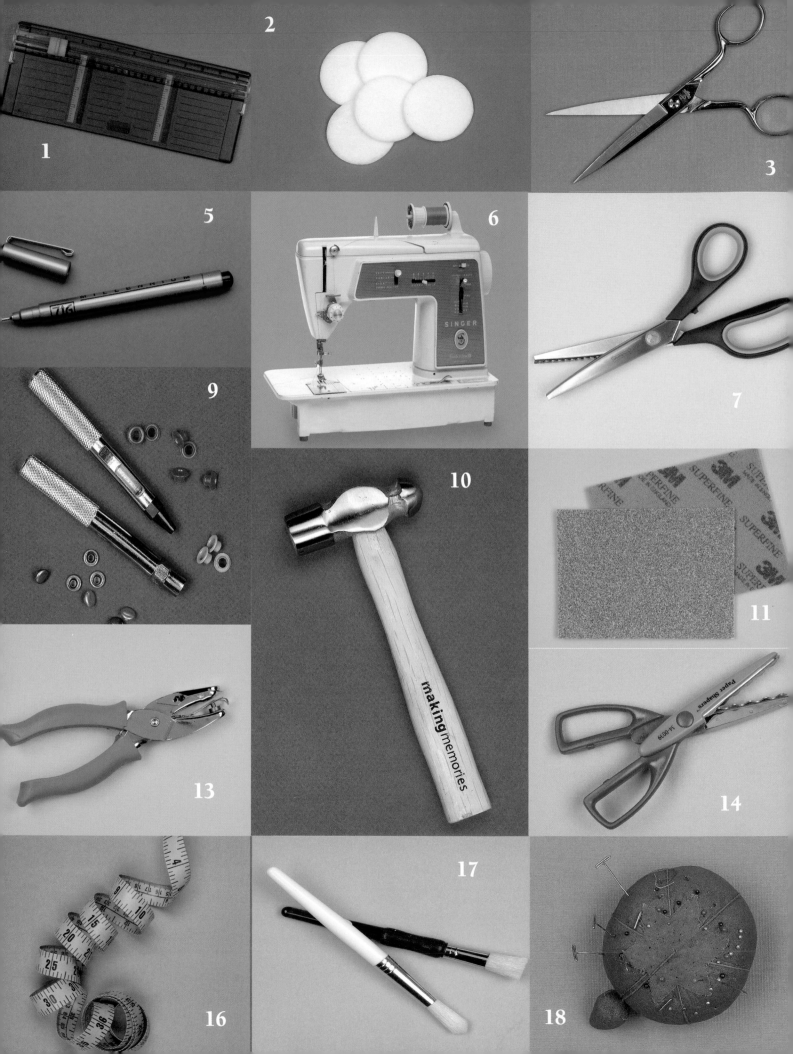

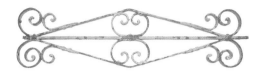

Chapter 1
SHABBY & BEYOND
TOOLS

1. Paper Cutter
2. FoofaLa Aging Sponges
3. Sharp Scissors
4. Markers
5. .05 Marker
6. Sewing Machine
7. Pinking Shears
8. Inking Stylus
9. Punch and Eyelet Setter
10. Hammer
11. Sandpaper
12. Xacto Knife
13. Hand-held Hole Punch

14. Decorative Scissors
15. Punches
16. Tape Measure
17. Paint Brushes for Stippling, Dry-Brush Technique, Painting Edges of Chip-board Letters & Paper
18. Needles
19. Fastenator
20. Dymo Labelmaker
21. Pencils
22. Corner Rounder
23. Bone Folder
24. Nail Files

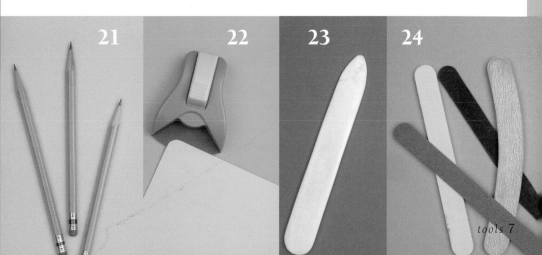

Materials on page 176

Chapter 2

SHABBY & BEYOND EMBELLISHMENTS

How can embellishments jazz up your layout?

1. **LETTERS:** Fun chipboard and pewter letters, scrabble wood tiles and metal words combine to make a mix of shabby, funky, bright, retro, vintage or chic titles.

2. **PAINTS AND INKS:** Use sandpaper to sand papers, tags, photos, chipboard letters or other embellishments, then slip-slap on acrylic paints (or inks) to distress and create rough and funky edges.

3. **SILK FLOWERS:** Add layered large and small silk flowers to your layout with vintage buttons or colorful brads for centers.

4. **CHIPBOARD DAISIES:** Spice up your page with hip pink chipboard daisies topped with buttons or brads, or try layering a small coordinating silk flower on your chipboard daisy with a sparkling rhinestone center to add pizazz.

5. **BUTTONS:** Large, small, tiny or antique buttons add dimension and a vintage feel to any layout. Bright, colorful, fancy, floral or snowflake buttons add a totally different flair.

6. **TAGS:** A theme throughout shabby scrapbooking: stain them, distress them, tear them, ink them, layer them, even crumple them. Whether they are large, small, itty bitty jewelry tags, white, colored, metal-rimmed, soft pastel or vellum tags, they add interest to your scrapbook page layouts. Tags are also perfect for titles, journaling and adhering small photos or additional embellishments to like wood clips, metal clips, keys, flowers, brads, buttons, metal letters and photo turns.

7. **BRADS:** There must be 500 ways to use the hundreds of brads available! Attach or hold photos, papers, memorabilia, mini files and ephemera in place; punch and insert into chipboard pieces, tags, letters and flowers or use as decoration just to add color.

8. **EYELETS:** Eyelets are not only wonderful color coordinated accessories for attaching items together but are also useful for threading ribbons, fibers, string, raffia, twill, trims and tulle.

9. **METAL LABEL HOLDERS:** Use oval, square, large and small, brass, silver, white and colored metal label holders for inserting names and dates. You can rub with acrylic paint, apply flowers and thread holes with ribbons, fibers or strings.

10. **PEWTER FRAMES:** The invention of these little pewter frames was ingenious. Use as is and insert a small picture, or frame a small portion of the main photo. Try applying acrylic paint and wipe partially off; let dry and wrap with ribbons on one side or add vintage buttons or flowers with colorful brads for centers. Spell a word or name with pewter tiles on the side or bottom of the frame.

Imagine! These are just a FEW ideas you will see throughout this book.
With all the embellishments out there to entice you,
there is NO LIMIT to what to use or how to use them! Get wild,
go funky, and most of all, have fun!

Chapter 3
SHABBY & BEYOND MATERIALS:
TRIMS, RIBBONS, RICK RACK,
RUB-ONS, SEWING GOODIES & TAGS

My Favorite Things GOODIES. One can never have enough! That's how I feel anyway. I wanted to do this layout to show the top ten items that are my "have to haves" right now. I enjoy using a variety of goodies and am almost always motivated to do my layouts using these.

The next two delicious scrapbook layouts on pages on 11 and 12 were created to inspire you! Just look at all the materials "calling to us" out there in the scrapbooking world. Don't they stir your creative juices? What a feast for the eyes!

These extraordinary layouts awaken all the senses; they are "touchy-feely" pages that almost sing with "yummy stuff;" ribbons, rick rack, trims, stencils, tags, rub-ons, stamps, inks, sewing notions, stencils, fabrics, felt, pom-poms, patterned and bright cardstock and fabulous color!

You know a scrapbook page is great when you have to touch it, and you know it is fantastic when you want to hug it. These pages are absolutely huggable! Kim Henkel designed them; her love of "Shabby & Beyond" scrapbooking is clearly visible! You can see how important image, color and texture are for visual stimulation, and it looks like she has a lot of fun creating with these elements.

We are going to show you how YOU TOO can use an eclectic collection of items such as these to put these layouts together in your own unique way. Since scrapbooking is an expression of your personality and comes from the heart, we hope you will pull from the favorite ideas you see in this book and come up with many huggable pages all your own!

Wouldn't you treasure being able to make and frame a page like the one below for your arts and crafts studio? Go ahead and have fun creating one for yourself with all your favorite goodies! Dig into your ribbon and button collections, pull out your tags, brads and tulle, find your rub-ons and papers, search for your rick rack and let loose to make a page just for you! Let your imagination guide you!

things I love
k.a.h.   Date may '05
1. rub ons
2. fonts
3. stickers
4. doo dads
5. cardstock
6. patterned paper
7. stamps
8. ink
9. stencils
10.
No.   color   Order of Importance

I ♥ stickers & RUB-ONS

ribbon

rick rack

goody goody g
gummy gumdrops

Tags
Tags
Name   and   MORE
REC'D   PROMISED   CHARGES
tags
tags

SEWING

goodies

Materials on page 176

11

Stamps, Stamps and More Stamps... I love stamps, all kinds and all sizes. I could easily do layout after layout with my favorite ones. It's fun just thinking about where, when and who I was with when I received each and every stamp. I have realized that I could never have enough of them. You know you love stamps when you even love the smell of the rubber. ~ Kim

Chapter 4
SHABBY AND BEYOND RUBBER STAMPS, TAGS, PAINTS & INKS

*R*ubber stamps are fabulous little rubber-etched "pieces of art" that can be used to embellish your scrapbook pages! *Shabby & Beyond Scrapbooking Ideas* will open up a whole new world for you and encourage you to incorporate stamping into your page layouts. It may seem like we are leading you out of your comfort zone with challenging new ideas, and that's exactly what we intend to do.

But, we believe you'll be pleasantly surprised and delighted by how images, alphabets, inks and paints add another fun dimension to your creations! Throughout the following pages you will see acrylic paints used with foam stamps to add an edgy, funky look to your words and titles. There are spirals, flourishes, fleur de lis images, a variety of alphabet styles and more, available for you to try.

You'll also notice how we love to stamp and distress tags and papers to look lovingly and comfortably "worn." One secret we learned from Kim Henkel is this: use a small round FoofaLa sponge pressed a few times onto a desired color of dye or pigment inkpad, then simply rub ink very lightly onto the textured papers and edges of tags to get a beautiful soft-edged, aged and distressed look! The top

texture, or "tooth" as it is called, picks up a hint of color and the paper takes on a somewhat ethereal, magical quality! Try it. Practice makes perfect and the rewards are worth it. Even the practice is fun. Using a stipple brush is another way to get a distressed or aged look. Just tap your stipple brush into your inkpad several times and then directly onto the paper. You may want onto do this a few times to get the desired results.

Different fonts are really trendy now! Collecting alphabet stamps in order to mix and match styles and sizes of fonts in tiles, names and words is quite an addicting hobby for scrapbooking enthusiasts today. Whether you use rubber or foam, ink or paint, fonts are fun to play with on your scrapbook layouts. They are an investment worth making and you will use them over and over again.

We like to use simple, whimsical, artsy or sometimes classic images like the ones on the previous page. To begin your rubber stamping adventure, try stamping a favorite image in colored ink on colored cardstock or tags and adhere to your page. Any image will do... just get started and have fun exploring a new avenue in crafting scrapbook page layouts!

KIM HENKEL

*K*im has been scrapbooking for three years. Her work has appeared in *Simple Scrapbooks, Memory Makers, Paper Crafts, Legacy* and several TweetyJill publications. As a child, Kim loved playing with paper… from paper dolls to stickers. She later discovered fabric, earned a degree in Fashion Merchandising, and made quilts for many years. Kim finds inspiration in simple things… a colorful restaurant menu, home decorating magazines, antique shop window displays, or even a new color combination. Her home reflects her love of handmade items and treasures from her favorite places. Dave, her husband, takes photographs for her and they travel all over Southern California searching for new locations to shoot. One of their favorites is steps away from their home on a pier overlooking the Pacific Ocean.

FLOWERS *Kim Henkel*

MATERIALS

INKPADS: BROWN: Local Craft Store

PAPERS: Cardstock by Bazzill Basics; Patterned Paper by Melissa Frances and BasicGrey

MARKERS: Size .05 Marking Pen: Local Craft Store

TAGS: Local Craft Store

METAL ITEMS: Dye Decorative Clip: Local Craft Store

RIBBONS: Ribbons, Velvet Cording and Rick Rack: Local Fabric Store

ADHESIVES: Decorative Tape by Heidi Swapp; Adhesive Squares by Hermafix; Wet Glue by Magic Scraps

OTHER: Photo Corner and Chipboard Letters by Heidi Swapp; Vintage Buttons

TOOLS: Nail File; Makeup Sponges

INSTRUCTIONS

1. Attach a large rectangular piece of patterned paper to 12" x 12" paper.
2. Cut two strips of cardstock 1/2" x 12".
3. Adhere strips to top and bottom of the layout.
4. Attach three photos and add a photo corner to one of them.
5. Add the other two photos to the page with decorative tape.
6. Tie a ribbon around a piece of cardstock approximately 1 1/2" x 12" and adhere to middle as shown.
7. Add pieces of decorative tape to page (pink and white polka-dots and striped).
8. Using nail file, lightly sand green chipboard letters and age using sponges and brown ink.
9. Adhere letters with wet glue to cardstock strip in middle of page.
10. Write quote on cardstock on right side of page.
11. Glue rick rack to top and bottom of page and adhere buttons as shown.
12. Write date and location on tag with marking pen.
13. Tie velvet cording onto tag and attach to page using a small metal clip.

flowers

Spring is nature's way of saying "Let's Party!"

by Robin Williams

Huntington Library: Rose Garden in Pasadena, CA November 2004

One of my favorite places to visit is the Huntington Library in Pasadena. I am always amazed at the beautiful flowers in bloom there, no matter what the season. I take my camera with me whenever I go, and I am grateful to be immersed in the beauty that surrounds this building.

REINA

Kim Henkel

This is a picture of my sweet cousin, Reina, who was about eighteen months old at the time. While visiting with her Nana and Grandpa, Nana decided to put foam rollers in her hair. I am sure that after Nana removed the rollers and Reina looked in the mirror, there were precious little giggles, dances and beautiful bouncing curls.

MATERIALS

DYE INKPADS: Pink: Local Craft Store

PAPERS: Patterned Paper by KI Memories; Cardstock: Local Craft Store

MARKERS: Size .05 Marking Pen: Local Craft Store

WORDS, LETTERS OR STICKERS: Alphabet Stickers by Chatterbox

TAGS: Local Craft Store

BUTTONS: Vintage Buttons: Local Antique Store

RIBBONS: Ribbons and Rick Rack: Local Craft Store

FABRICS: Tulle: Local Fabric Store

ADHESIVES: Wet Glue by Magic Scraps; Adhesive Squares by Hermafix

OTHER: Small Red Chipboard Heart and Photo Corners by Heidi Swapp

INSTRUCTIONS

1. Adhere photo to center of page, adding photo corners.
2. Cut several brightly colored cardstocks and patterned papers in strips to frame photo.
3. Tie ribbons, tulle and rick rack around strips.
4. Adhere strips to page to frame photo and glue buttons to ends of strips.
5. Cut a small piece of cardstock for title. Add stickers to cardstock to spell out name or title around right side of title block.
6. Add cardstock heart under ribbon and glue in place.
7. Attach title to page under photo.
8. Write journaling on aged, inked tag using marking pen. Tie a piece of ribbon to tag and adhere to page.

My husband and I planned a trip to the Grand Canyon in February of 2004... little did we know the weather would be so unbearable. We didn't bring the right clothes. Off to the store we went to buy a few items to keep us warm... hats, gloves and scarves. Once we had on our new purchases and were a tad warmer, I said to my husband, "I have my hat, my gloves and my scarf... I'm ready to go." He replied, "I am too because I have my hat, my gloves, my scarf and my love." A memory I will cherish forever!

MY LOVE

Kim Henkel

MATERIALS

RUBBER STAMPS: Alphabet from All Night Media/Plaid by Brenda Walton; Tag by All Night Media/Plaid; Star by Paper Inspirations

PIGMENT INKPADS: Browns, Rust and Black: Local Craft Store

PAPERS: Gold Cardstock: Local Craft Store

MARKERS: Size .05 Marking Pen: Local Craft Store

WORDS, LETTERS OR STICKERS: License Plate Alphabet Stickers by Paper Loft; Alphabet Stickers by Sticker Studio and Wordsworth; 3-Dimensional Letter Stickers by EK Success; FoofaBets by FoofaLa

TAGS: Local Craft Store

METAL ITEMS: Black Metal Photo Anchors by 7gypsies; Metal Alphabet Stencils by Li'l Davis Designs; Straight Pins by Making Memories

FABRICS: Plaid Fabric: Local Fabric Store; Wool Felt: Local Antique or Fabric Store; Rick Rack: Local Craft or Fabric Store

ADHESIVES: Hermafix; Scrappy Glue by Magic Scraps

OTHER: Embroidery Needle and Floss; Vintage Flash Card

TOOLS: Sewing Machine; Pinking Shears by Mundial

INSTRUCTIONS

1. Tear a piece of fabric to cover most of a sheet of 12"x 12" gold cardstock.

2. Tape fabric in place with removable tape; stitch down using a sewing machine, creating a crosshatch pattern as if you were making a quilt.

3. Use pinking shears to cut a piece of wool felt; cut a little askew to add character. Hand-sew a decorative stitch with embroidery floss for photo mat.

4. Use two photo anchors to attach your photo to wool felt. Hand-stitch the photo anchors in place with embroidery floss.

5. Attach wool felt to background fabric using small dots of Scrappy Glue.

6. Stamp image of tag and star on small rectangle of cardstock and hand-write journaling with .05 marking pen. Trim one side of tag image with pinking shears and attach to wool felt using a straight pin.

7. Hand-write date on small tag using .05 marking pen and pin to wool felt.

8. Choose your favorite letters, stickers and rubber stamps to create journaling on vintage flash card.

9. Embellish with rick rack.

DAWNE & WALLY: BEST FRIENDS

Kim Henkel

MATERIALS

RUBBER STAMPS: Birthday-Sept. 2003 by Making Memories; Yardstick by Limited Edition Rubber Stamps

DYE INKPADS: Browns and Green: Local Craft Store

PAPERS: Mustard, Red and Light Green Cardstock and Lined School Paper: Local Craft Store

MARKERS: Size .05 Marking Pen: Local Craft Store

COMPUTER FONTS: Two Peas in a Bucket

WORDS, LETTERS OR STICKERS: Bottle Cap Stickers and Skeleton Key Sticker by EK Success

TAGS: Local Craft Store

METAL ITEMS: Round Paper Clip by 7gypsies; Straight Pins: Local Craft Store

BUTTONS: Vintage Buttons: Local Antique Store

FIBERS: Local Craft or Fabric Store

FABRICS: Local Fabric Store or Quilt Shop

ADHESIVES: Adhesive Squares by Herma-fix; Glue Dots by Glue Dots International

OTHER: Large Playing Card; Embroidery Floss; Linen Thread

TOOLS: Sewing Machine; Aging Sponge by FoofaLa; Embroidery Needle; Stipple Brush

INSTRUCTIONS

1. Print photos on photo printer in black and white.

2. Adhere a strip of light green cardstock to top of page using adhesive squares.

3. Tear a piece of fabric approximately 4" x 10".

4. Use sewing machine to stitch fabric to cardstock, sewing only sides and bottom; leave top open for a pocket. Stitch down middle of fabric pocket.

5. Use marking pen to write "best friends" on muslin, then stitch over using needle and embroidery thread. Tear "best friends" section out of muslin, taking care not to tear too close.

6. Randomly stitch "best friends" piece to fabric pocket.

7. Cut cardstock and slip in pocket.

8. Attach photos to cardstock.

9. Stamp yardstick image on another piece of cardstock using green ink; age stamped image using brown ink and FoofaLa sponge.

10. Adhere stamped image to playing card with round paper clip. Wrap embroidery floss around card and stamped image several times and tie in a bow.

11. Slide card in fabric pocket and use a Glue Dot to hold in place.

12. Add journaling to lined paper and age using sponge and brown ink; add several stickers of your choice.

13. Use a stipple brush to add a touch of green ink to journaling paper.

14. Adhere journaling to piece of mustard colored cardstock; slip it on pocket.

15. Write the title on tag; add date to page with birthday stamp; add fiber and buttons and attach to fabric pocket with straight pins.

This picture is of my friend Dawne and her beloved dog Wally. Not long after I finished this layout, Wally became ill and passed away. I am so glad that I created this layout because it shows how happy Dawne was when Wally was here. He may have been just a dog to many, but he was Dawne's best friend. Wally, you will always be remembered.

I love this photo of my mom on her birthday, enjoying an ice cream sundae. I added the handkerchief to this page because it reminds me so much of her. When I was little, she always made sure that I had my own small-sized hankies. She even embroidered my initials in one corner. This page really makes me smile when I see how happy she is.

HAPPY BIRTHDAY MOM

Kim Henkel

MATERIALS

RUBBER STAMPS: Alphabet from All Night Media/Plaid by Brenda Walton; Deco Border by Penny Black; Heart by Claudia Rose; Happy Birthday by Rubber Monger

PIGMENT INKPADS: Black, Red, Blue and Browns: Local Craft Store

PAPERS: Patterned Paper and Turquoise and Pink Cardstock by KI Memories; Patterned Specialty Paper and Cardstock: Local Craft Store

MARKERS: Size .05 Marking Pen: Local Craft Store

WORDS, LETTERS OR STICKERS: FoofaBets by FoofaLa

TAGS: Tag by FoofaLa; Small Jewelry Tag: Local Craft Store

METAL ITEMS: Metal Clip by 7gypsies

BUTTONS: Local Antique Store

RIBBONS: Assorted Ribbons: Local Craft Store; Lace Trim: Local Antique Store

FABRICS: Cotton Muslin: Local Craft or Fabric Store

ADHESIVES: Hermafix; Scrappy Glue by Magic Scraps

OTHER: Library Card; Blue Envelope; Quilting Thread and Embroidery Floss; Vintage Handkerchief; Flower Embellishment by Li'l Davis Designs

TOOLS: Pinking Shears by Mundial; Aging Sponges by FoofaLa

INSTRUCTIONS

1. Cut several pieces of cardstock and patterned paper to create a paper quilt for your background, as shown.

2. Use pinking shears to add decorative edges here and there on the background quilt pieces.

3. Add rubber stamp images to a couple of different background pieces.

4. Attach photo to the right side of page.

5. Tear a piece of cotton muslin into a small rectangle. Using embroidery floss, stitch a primitive running stitch around edge of muslin piece and adhere to bottom with small dots of Scrappy Glue.

6. Cut a rectangular piece of cardstock; age using FoofaLa sponges and pigment ink. Stamp heart image and "happy birthday" and attach to page. Glue button to cardstock under heart stamped image.

7. Cut out "MOM" from FoofaLa FoofaBets and attach to cardstock.

8. Age edges of envelope using FoofaLa sponges and brown pigment inks.

9. Attach a strip of patterned paper to envelope.

10. Tie various pieces of ribbon and lace trim around envelope.

11. Sew button to top piece of ribbon using quilting thread.

12. Hand-write the date on the shipping tag and attach tag to one of the ribbons on the envelope. Insert vintage handkerchief into envelope.

13. Stamp birthday image onto library card.

14. Hand-write "with all my heart" on top of library card and glue on flower embellishment using Scrappy Glue.

15. Hand-write "candles", "presents", "wishes", "love" and "xoxo" on piece of cardstock and attach to left side of page.

XOXO

Kim Henkel

My husband and I like to visit a beautiful, little farm in San Diego. We wonder how we would like to live on a farm. But, whenever we hear my grandmother talk about how much work she had to do when she lived on a farm, growing up in a small town in Illinois, we quickly reconsider and appreciate how fortunate we are to live at the beach.

MATERIALS

RUBBER STAMPS: Gothic Lowercase Alphabet by Postmodern Design; Flower by Paper Inspirations

PIGMENT INKPADS: Black: Local Craft Store

DYE INKPADS: Brown and Chartreuse: Local Craft Store

PAPERS: Green Geometric and Blue and Green Dot by KI Memories; Stripes and Polka-Dots by SEI; Cardstock and Green Gingham: Local Craft Store

WORDS, LETTERS OR STICKERS: Alphabet Stickers by Wordsworth, KI Memories and Rusty Pickle

RUB-ONS: Rub-On Alphabets by Li'l Davis Designs

TAGS: Local Craft Store

RIBBONS: Ribbons and Rick Rack: Local Craft Store; Twill by 7gypsies

ADHESIVES: Adhesive Squares by Hermafix; Glue Lines by Glue Dots International

TOOLS: Corner Rounder by Marvy Uchida; Pinking Shears by Mundial

INSTRUCTIONS

1. Use several different alphabet stickers/rub-ons for "XOXO" on tags.
2. Add ribbons and rick rack to tags.
3. Cut differently sized patterned papers to go behind the tags and letters.
4. Use corner rounder on all patterned papers.
5. Attach patterned papers, tags and photos to cardstock.
6. Cut a strip of cardstock approximately 1 ½" x 10".
7. Use corner rounder on one side of the strip of cardstock and pinking shears on the other.
8. Tie ribbons around strip.
9. Adhere strip to cardstock using Glue Lines.

My mom told me this was the first time she had ever been on vacation. My grandfather wanted to get a picture of my uncle, my mom and my grandmother in front of the Arizona sign. Don't you just love those cowboy hats? Yee-haw!

FIRST FAMILY VACATION

Kim Henkel

MATERIALS

RUBBER STAMPS: Clock Stamps by Postmodern Design; Tag by Inkadinkado Rubber Stamps

PIGMENT INKPADS: Medium and Dark Brown: Local Craft Store

PIGMENT INK: Black: Local Craft Store

PAPERS: Map Patterned Paper by K&Company; Address Book Patterned Paper by Making Memories; Various Colors of Cardstock by Bazzill Basics; FoofaBets and Dictionary Definitions by FoofaLa

WORDS, LETTERS OR STICKERS: Alphabet Stickers by Rusty Pickle

RUB-ONS: Alphabet Rub-Ons by Making Memories

METAL ITEMS: Metal Handle by FoofaLa

FIBERS: FoofaLa

BUTTONS: Local Antique Store

RIBBONS: Various Ribbons: Local Craft Store; Rick Rack: Local Antique Store

ADHESIVES: Hermafix; Scrappy Glue by Magic Scraps

TOOLS: Pinking Shears by Mundial; Small Hole Punch; Aging Sponge by FoofaLa

INSTRUCTIONS

1. Attach map paper to top of medium brown cardstock.

2. Cut four squares of differently colored cardstock in various sizes and randomly cut sides using pinking shears; attach to cardstock under map paper.

3. Print a vintage vacation photo using a photo printer and sepia tones.

4. Mat photo using dark brown cardstock and attach to map paper; be sure to tilt photo slightly to give a collage-like feel to your page.

5. Age several FoofaLa definitions using FoofaLa aging sponges and brown inkpad.

6. Punch holes in definitions and adhere randomly to cardstock on bottom of page using various ribbons.

7. Adhere one small pinked piece of teal cardstock and add an embellishment - shown here is a small FoofaLa handle adhered with Scrappy Glue.

8. Use pinking shears to cut a small piece of deep red cardstock and attach to title square

with ribbon. Add an embellishment of your choice.

9. Using a tag stamp and black ink, stamp image on ledger paper. Trim one side of ledger paper using pinking shears. Hand-write family name in the stamped image. Attach ledger paper to gold and adhere to page. Add three buttons.

10. Pink red title square and apply white alphabet rub-ons to spell out "First Family Vacation"; punch hole and add a piece of rick rack and a button.

11. Using black stamp ink and a clock stamp of your choice, stamp image on address paper. Use various alphabet stickers to spell out "Sun Time".

12. Attach clock and "Sun Time" address paper to teal cardstock piece and add to page.

13. Cut out numbers indicating the year the photo was taken and attach to olive green piece of cardstock; adhere to layout.

14. Use Scrappy Glue to adhere vintage buttons to definitions to add a finishing touch to your page.

FOREVER & EVER

Kim Henkel

MATERIALS

RUBBER STAMPS: Chunky Alphabet and Gothic Lower Alphabet by Postmodern Design; Tall Alphabet by Stampotique Originals; Mara-Mi Alphabet by Hampton Art; XOXO Heart by Paper Inspirations; Art Heart by American Art Stamp; Heart Bull's-Eye by Savvy Stamps

PIGMENT INKPADS: Black: Local Craft Store

DYE INKPADS: Red, Sepia and Coffee: Local Craft Store

PAPERS: Red, Cream and Turquoise Cardstock: Local Craft Store

WORDS, LETTERS OR STICKERS: Jumbo Letter Stickers (Black) by Chatterbox; Tailored Letters (Red) by Scrapworks

RUB-ONS: Mixed Up and Heidi (Black) by Making Memories; Expressions (Beetle Black) by Doodlebug Design; Alphabet (Black) by Li'l Davis Designs

TAGS: Local Craft Store or Office Supply

METAL ITEMS: Black Eyelets: Local Craft Store

RIBBONS: Local Craft Store

FABRICS: Turquoise Tulle: Local Fabric Store

ADHESIVES: Adhesive Squares by Hermafix

OTHER: Green Library Pocket by Li'l Davis Designs

TOOLS: Pinking Shears by Mundial; Corner Rounder by Marvy Uchida

This is one of my favorite pictures of me and my husband Dave. I love using different kinds of rub-ons, and had lots of fun with such a variety. I wanted to show my love for my husband, knowing that we will be together "forever." He agrees!

INSTRUCTIONS

1. Cut three 10" strips of cream cardstock.

2. Use a corner rounder to shape one end of each strip; use pinking shears on the other end of the strip.

3. Apply a variety of different rub-ons, stickers and alphabet stamps for your saying.

4. Use Hermafix squares to adhere the three strips to the top of the red cardstock.

5. Cut a piece of turquoise cardstock slightly larger than your photo; trim with pinking shears on the left side. Set five eyelets in cardstock for your ribbons. Slip ribbons through and tie.

6. Use corner rounder on one corner of photo.

7. Stamp hearts on all three tags. Tie ribbons on two tags.

8. Adhere green library card pocket to the right side of photo and add tags to the inside of the pocket.

9. Tie velvet ribbon around the library card pocket.

10. Tie tulle through the metal-rimmed tag and attach under velvet ribbon.

1956

Kim Henkel

These pictures are of my grandmother when she was in her mid-twenties. She had just received this Mix Master for her birthday. She is the best cook I have ever known, and we still enjoy her recipes today. My favorites are her homemade noodles, rice meatballs and "gobs" cookies. I used muted colors in this layout because they match the ones in my grandma's sundress.

MATERIALS

RUBBER STAMPS: Flower and Gingham Check by Paper Inspirations; Harlequin by Judi-Kins; Tape Measure by Stampotique Originals

DYE INKPADS: Brown, Olive and Mustard: Local Craft Store

PAPERS: Striped Paper by 7gypsies; Floral by Daisy D's; Cardstock: Local Craft Store

TAGS: Local Craft Store or Office Supply

METAL ITEMS: Decorative Brads, Eyelets and Paper Clip: Local Craft Store

RIBBONS: Local Craft or Fabric Store

FABRICS: Wool: Local Antique Store; Tulle: Local Fabric Store

ADHESIVES: Adhesive Squares by Hermafix; Glue Dots and Glue Lines by Glue Dots International

OTHER: Miss Muffet Label by Melissa Frances; Mini File Folder by FoofaLa; Cardboard Number Stencils

TOOLS: Dymo Labelmaker; Pinking Shears by Mundial

INSTRUCTIONS

1. Add large pieces of patterned paper to 12" x 12" black cardstock.

2. Mat photos with black cardstock; trim top of one piece of black cardstock with pinking shears.

3. Type recipe and adhere to inside of mini file folder.

4. Decorate front of file folder with patterned paper, brads, paper clip and tulle. Add Dymo tape to side of mini folder recipe.

5. Attach photos and mini file folder to top of page.

6. Stamp images on top of "1956" stencils and adhere eyelets randomly to stencils.

7. Tie stencils together using ribbons and fibers of your choice. Glue pieces of cardstock behind the stencils for support.

8. Attach wool pieces to cardstock using Glue Lines.

9. Add saying to top and sides of stencils using Dymo tape.

10. Adhere stencils to top of wool pieces on the bottom of the layout.

11. Stamp "XOXO" to tag and attach to bottom right corner of page, on top of the "6" stencil.

MY GRANDMA 1 9 5 G BAKER/COOK I HAVE EVER KNOWN!

THE BEST

XOXO

Ask not what your country can do for you, but what you can do for **YOUR** country!
John F. Kennedy

US navy

My brother Gary days before leaving to fight for our country! I'm so proud of you!

This is a picture of my brother right before he was deployed.
Our family is so proud of all of his accomplishments in the military.

ASK NOT WHAT YOU CAN DO FOR YOUR COUNTRY...

Kim Henkel

MATERIALS

PAPERS: Cardstock: Local Craft Store; Patterned Paper by 7gypsies

COMPUTER FONTS: Two Peas in a Bucket

WORDS, LETTERS OR STICKERS: Epoxy Letters by Creative Imaginations

TAGS: Local Craft Store

TRANSPARENCIES: Local Office Supply

METAL ITEMS: Metal Letters and Photo Corners by Making Memories

RIBBONS: Rick Rack: Local Fabric Store

ADHESIVES: Wet Glue by Magic Scraps; Adhesive Squares by Hermafix; Glue Dots by Glue Dots International

OTHER: Star Charm; Linen Thread; Stamps and Military Bar Pin from Local Antique Store; Walnut Ink Spray

TOOLS: Sewing Machine

INSTRUCTIONS

1. Cut four strips of red cardstock approximately 1 ¼" wide by 12" long.

2. Attach red strips to cardstock as shown.

3. Use your sewing machine to create a running stitch around page, approximately one inch from edge.

4. Attach photo to right side of page and glue on metal photo corners.

5. Cut a piece of patterned paper for left side of photo and attach to cardstock.

6. Type journaling and print on transparency (for top and bottom of page). Leave a space to add "YOUR" epoxy stickers on the journaling.

7. Attach transparency to top and bottom of layout using Glue Dots under photo, so you do not see the Glue Dots through the transparency. Glue stamps to sides of transparency.

8. Tag: Use walnut ink and follow manufacturer's directions to age tag. Decorate tag with military bar pin and metal letters. Attach star charm to linen thread; tie on tag and adhere to page layout.

THE ROBINSON FAMILY
Kim Henkel

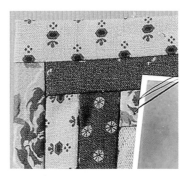

MATERIALS

RUBBER STAMPS: Polka Dots by Stampotique Originals

PIGMENT INKPADS: Coffee, Sepia, Green and Burgundy: Local Craft Store

PAPERS: Green and Brown Cardstock: Local Craft Store

WORDS, LETTERS OR STICKERS: FoofaBets by FoofaLa

RUB-ONS: Alphabet and Numbers by Making Memories

TAGS: Mini Black Tag by FoofaLa; Large Shipping Tag by 7gypsies

RIBBONS: Black Velvet Ribbon and Satin Ribbon from Local Craft or Fabric Store

FABRICS: 100% Cotton Fabric: Local Fabric Store

ADHESIVES: Hermafix; Scrappy Glue by Magic Scraps

OTHER: Clock Accent by Li'l Davis Designs; Straight Pin; Walnut Ink Spray

TOOLS: Pinking Shears by Mundial; Aging Sponges by FoofaLa; Iron

INSTRUCTIONS

1. Use various pieces of quilting fabric to create a log cabin quilt block as a mat for your vintage photo. To create quilt block, cut strips of fabric 1 ¼" wide. Cut center square large enough for your photo. Use sewing machine to stitch fabric strips to the center square, trimming strips as you sew. Continue sewing until you have three strips of fabric all the way around. Press quilt block with an iron.

2. Fold and iron ¼" of fabric around outside edge of quilt block to the back of the block, in order to prevent seeing the raw edge of fabric. Glue to page with Scrappy Glue.

3. Print out sepia-toned photo from computer.

4. Sew photo to quilt block with quilting thread. Add a Hermafix tab to the back of page to hold the thread down. Adhere a small piece of cardstock on top of Hermafix.

5. Using black number rub-ons, indicate year photo was taken on a small black tag. Attach to quilt block with straight pin.

6. Stamp background in green ink on walnut-stained tag.

7. Apply black alphabet rub-ons to spell out "The" and "Family" on small pieces of green cardstock. Trim sides of cardstock using pinking shears.

8. Age the FoofaBets using sponges with coffee and sepia inks. Use brown cardstock and aged Foofa-Bets to spell your family name.

9. Attach "The", (family name), and "Family" to stained tag and tie on satin ribbon.

10. Punch eight small holes on bottom of tag. Thread and tie with black velvet ribbon, cutting off excess.

11. Add clock embellishment to tag and attach to bottom of page.

A classic quilt square was used for my vintage family photo. The rich green and wine colors remind me of the 1940's era. This photo is of my grandfather (top row second from left) and his family when he recently joined the air force. Doesn't he look so proud to be standing next to his brother, who was also in the military?!

CUTE AS A BUTTON

Kim Henkel

MATERIALS

DYE INKPADS: Red: Local Craft Store

PAPERS: Cardstock by Doodlebug Design; Patterned Papers by MOD from Autumn Leaves, Collage Press and Cross My Heart; Scalloped Paper by K&Company

MARKERS: Size .05 Marking Pen: Local Craft Store

RUB-ONS: Alphabet Rub-Ons by KI Memories

TAGS: Local Craft Store

RIBBONS: Local Craft Store

FABRICS: Tulle: Local Fabric Store

ADHESIVES: Adhesive Squares by Hermafix; Glue Lines and Glue Dots by Glue Dots International

OTHER: Safety Pin; Antique Buttons; Packing String

TOOLS: Makeup Sponge

Lilly's sister, Ava, is the newest addition to our extended family. She was born prematurely, and when I saw her for the first time, I couldn't help but think how cute and tiny she was. It inspired me to do this layout, "Cute as a Button."

INSTRUCTIONS

1. Ink scalloped paper with sponge and ink; adhere scalloped paper to cardstock.
2. Mat photos using patterned papers.
3. Attach matted photos to scalloped paper as shown.
4. Tie ribbon and tulle through buttons and attach to top of page with Glue Dots.
5. Tie ribbon around page and secure with a Glue Dot.
6. Apply alphabet rub-ons to spell out "Cute as a Button".
7. Write baby details on tag and attach to orange ribbon.
8. Add several buttons to string; tie around a safety pin and attach to the orange ribbon.

Sweet Avaleigh
born 3.20.09
4 lbs. 8oz.

CUTE as a Button

"I **love** you Davey!"

why you ask!

"I **love** you because...

You know I love shrimp and hate mustard!
You love animals!
You tell me to have a good day when I go to work!
You love Disneyland as much as I do!
You know how to cook...and you love to do it!
You know how to clean a 'mean' sink!
You have a green thumb!
You like to visit the San Diego Zoo & the Wild Animal Park!

You like to get pedicures!
You remind me who got wet at our beach BBQ 3 years ago!
You love my cold feet in bed!
You always tell me what looks best!
You named our first orchid 'Sid'!
You know my favorite flower!
You are spontaneous!
You surprise me! I love surprises!

You said, 'I do' on April 19, 2000!
Happy Second Anniversary My Love!

Key
to
my
heart

WHY I LOVE YOU

Kim Henkel

MATERIALS

RUBBER STAMPS: Alphabet by Wordsworth

PAPERS: Celery and Beige Cardstock: Local Craft Store; Wine Velvet Paper: Local Craft Store

COMPUTER FONT: Jack Frost by Two Peas in a Bucket

METAL ITEMS: Key and Metal Heart: Local Antique Store or Flea Market

ADHESIVES: Hermafix; Scrappy Glue by Magic Scraps

FABRICS: 100% Cotton Osnaburg Fab-

ric: Local Fabric Store

TAGS: Small Tag Die Cut by Quickutz from Provo Craft; Large Tag by Paper Reflections/DMD Industries

OTHER: Fiber; Embroidery Floss; Walnut Ink from Local Craft Store; Crocheted Squares from Local Antique Store; Walnut Ink Spray

TOOLS: Embroidery Needle

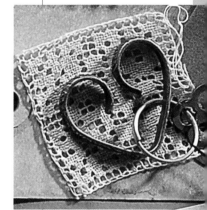

INSTRUCTIONS

1. Use celery-colored cardstock as your background.

2. Tear a piece of fabric for your photo mat.

3. Hand-sew a primitive running stitch around the edge of fabric with three strands of embroidery floss; leave room for your photo.

4. Sew photo in place using large stitches in embroidery floss on the corners of photo, as shown.

5. Place several small dots of Scrappy Glue on back of osnaburg fabric; adhere photo to the front.

6. Glue photo and fabric to a pre-cut piece of wine velvet paper and adhere to cardstock.

7. Age a piece of cardstock with walnut ink and place on background cardstock on left side of page.

8. Cut a strip of wine velvet paper and attach to bottom of page as shown.

9. Using computer fonts, print journaling; cut out several different sizes and attach to page.

10. Age a small shipping tag with walnut ink and print "key to my heart" using computer fonts.

11. Decorate a walnut-stained shipping tag with antique findings such as a metal heart, skeleton key and crocheted square.

12. Thread ribbon or fibers through shipping tag and attach to page; add a thread to connect them.

My husband Davey is always teasing me and asking me, "Why do you love me?"

So, just for fun and to let him know why, I created this srapbook page just for him.

THAT'S AMORE

Kim Henkel

MATERIALS

RUBBER STAMPS: ABC by Stampers Anonymous; Alphabet by Postmodern Design

DYE INKPADS: Brown and Green: Local Craft Store

PAPERS: Cardstock: Local Craft Store; Patterned Papers by Melissa Frances; Square Scalloped Card and Envelope by Paper Source

MARKERS: Size .05 Marking Pen: Local Craft Store

COLORED PENCILS: Watercolor Pencil (Red): Local Craft Store

WORDS, LETTERS OR STICKERS: Alphabet Stickers by Scrapworks, Chatterbox and KI Memories

RUB-ONS: Melissa Frances and KI Memories

TAGS: DMD Industries and American Tag

RIBBONS: Local Craft and Fabric Store

ADHESIVES: Adhesive Squares by Hermafix; Glue Dots and Glue Lines by Glue Dots International

OTHER: Red and White String; Paper Clip; Flash Card

TOOLS: Aging Sponge by FoofaLa; Heart Punch by Paper Source; Compass, Protractor or Kitchen Bowl

INSTRUCTIONS

1. Cut three rectangular strips in various sizes from patterned paper; attach to 12" x 12" piece of red cardstock.

2. Stamp alphabet on flash card in green ink and adhere to page.

3. Adhere vellum envelope and scalloped-cut card to page.

4. Cut a small strip of blue cardstock. Punch out a heart from blue cardstock and adhere strip to top of scalloped card.

5. Use rub-ons for title on card and on blue cardstock strip.

6. Color in heart rub-on with red pencil.

7. Using a compass, protractor or kitchen bowl, trace large circle (pizza shape) on patterned paper. Cut out and adhere to page as shown.

8. Tie a piece of ribbon to a red shipping tag and attach to top of circle.

9. Tie a piece of ribbon to a small round tag and attach to bottom of circle.

10. Use rub-ons and alphabet stickers to journal onto the pizza circle, red shipping tag and round tag.

11. Attach photo to bottom of layout.

12. Cut out a triangle (shape of a pizza slice) from the same patterned paper you used for your pizza circle. Tie string around paper clip and add to bottom of page to hold photo and pizza slice on your page.

13. Age all papers with sponge and brown ink.

My husband and I used to live near a wonderful Italian restaurant called Pompeii. We hadn't been there in years and happened to be in the area, so we decided to go to relive some of our first dates. Everything was exactly the way we remembered it… right down to the waitresses.

41

SIMPLE PLEASURES OF SUMMER

Kim Henkel

These pages remind me of the wonderful time that my husband and I spent in Arizona. Little did we know how much we would enjoy the "simple pleasures" that we found in the desert. We were amazed by its beauty and look forward to our next trip there.

MATERIALS

RUBBER STAMPS: Date Stamp by Making Memories; Fleur de Lis: Local Craft Store

DYE INKPADS: Black and Brown: Local Craft Store

PAPERS: Cardstock: Local Craft Store

COMPUTER FONTS: Two Peas in a Bucket

TAGS: DMD Industries and American Tag

TRANSPARENCIES: Local Craft Store

ADHESIVES: Adhesive Squares by Hermafix; Wet Glue by Magic Scraps

OTHER: Round Metal Clip; Leather Cording and Fibers; Vintage Buttons; Embroidery Floss; Canvas Photo Paper; Handmade Paper

TOOLS: Embroidery Needle; Aging Sponge by FoofaLa

INSTRUCTIONS

1. Tear the top of two pieces of gold 12" x 12" cardstock.
2. Tear them again, creating a small opening for a piece of tan cardstock to show through.
3. Adhere tan cardstock to the back of the torn cardstock with adhesive squares. Primitively stitch the two pieces of cardstock together with embroidery floss as shown.
4. Use a computer-generated font to spell out title; print and cut out.
5. Add the title and photos under embroidered floss.
6. Write different words on several jewelry tags and attach tags to the embroidery floss.
7. Print two photos on canvas paper and mat using brown handmade paper; make one mat larger than photo to leave room for the antique buttons. Tear the photo mat on one of the matted photos.
8. Adhere the photos to both sides of the layouts.
9. Stamp fleur de lis image on large tag.
10. Decorate the large tag using the second canvas photo and pieces of handmade paper. Tie cording through tag and add to left side of page.
11. Add two more photos to right side of layout and hand-stitch antique buttons in between them.
12. Tie a piece of leather cording around canvas photo on right side of layout as shown.
13. Age all papers using sponge and brown ink.

TWINS

Kim Henkel

MATERIALS

DYE INKPADS: Brown and Pink: Local Craft Store

PAPERS: Patterned Papers by KI Memories, Cardstock from Local Craft Store; Large Paper Circles by Paper Source

RUB-ONS: Alphabet by KI Memories

TAGS: Local Craft Store

METAL ITEMS: Eyelets by Doodlebug Design; Plain Clip and Blue Clip: Local Craft Store

RIBBONS: Beaux Regards

FABRICS: Printed Twill by 7 Gypsies; Scalloped and Zigzag Felt Strips by Paper Source; Plain Twill: Local Craft Store

ADHESIVES: Adhesive Squares by Hermafix, Wet Glue by Magic Scraps

OTHER: Clothespin; Chipboard Letters and Hearts by Heidi Swapp

TOOLS: Nail File; Circle Punch by Marvy Uchida; Aging Sponges by FoofaLa

INSTRUCTIONS

1. Cut two squares of patterned paper and adhere them diagonally across from two photos, on the opposite corners of the page as shown.

2. Punch three small circles from patterned paper and adhere to top right side of page.

3. Use nail file to lightly sand chipboard letters and hearts. Sponge letters with pink ink to add color; use brown ink after the pink to age.

4. Tie a ribbon around largest heart and glue all hearts to small circles.

5. Once they are dry, glue letters to large paper circle. Set five eyelets above chipboard letter title "Twins" and five below. Run twill through eyelets and tie ends as shown.

6. Use marking pen to write date and location on tag. Attach tag to bottom of large circle with clip.

7. Write children's names on tags using rub-ons; glue felt strips to tags. Tie ribbon through tags and attach to page with clothespin and metal clip as shown.

Every year, my husband and I plan a trip to Palm Springs with our best friends, Ron and Pam. Last year, we had double the fun, because our time together included Ron and Pam's twins, Rachael and Natalie. I loved watching the interaction between the two little girls, and thinking about what wonderful and playful friends they will be for each other while growing up.

LILLY'S FIRST MOVIE

Kim Henkel

MATERIALS

RUBBER STAMPS: Large Flower by Stampotique Originals

DYE INKPADS: Pink and Brown: Local Craft Store

PAPERS: Off-White, Pink, Purple, Yellow, Melon, Lavender and Lime Green Cardstock: Local Craft Store

WORDS, LETTERS OR STICK-ERS: Purple Jumbo Letter Stickers by Chatterbox

RUB-ONS: Expressions by Doodlebug Design

TAGS: Local Craft Store

RIBBONS: Ribbons and Green Rick Rack: Local Craft Store

FABRICS: Pink Fabric and Tulle: Local Craft or Fabric Store

ADHESIVES: Adhesive Squares by Hermafix; Glue Dots by Glue Dots International

OTHER: Pink and Turquoise Embroidery Floss

TOOLS: Embroidery Needle

INSTRUCTIONS

1. Tear a piece of pink homespun fabric into a 10" x 10" square.

2. Hand-sew a running stitch around the edge of pink fabric using turquoise embroidery thread. Adhere fabric to cardstock.

3. Hand-cut primitive shaped flowers, flower centers and leaves from cardstock.

4. Adhere the photo under one of the flowers and on top of the fabric as shown.

5. Cut three long strips of rick rack for flower stems.

6. Adhere and assemble flowers, stems and leaves to fabric as shown.

7. Glue green rick rack on top of flower stems and tie on small pieces of pink tulle.

8. Use alphabet rub-ons on raffle tickets and adhere to bottom of photo.

9. Use stickers to spell name on mini envelope.

10 Use pink ink to stamp flower on tag; use alphabet rub-ons for wording on tag. Add ribbon.

11. Adhere envelope and tag to fabric; use embroidery floss to add detail. Use rub-ons to add date to a small tag and attach it to envelope.

I love taking pictures of my niece Lilly. On this day, Lilly's grandmother and I decided to take Lilly to see her first movie, "Winnie the Pooh", at the theater. We were delighted to see how interested and excited Lilly was as she watched the big screen. We were also amazed at how much she enjoyed her soft drink, which was about as big as she was.

THINGS AROUND THE HOUSE...

Kim Henkel

MATERIALS

PIGMENT INK: Red: Local Craft Store

PAPERS: Cardstock by Bazzill Basics

COMPUTER FONTS: David Walker/Two Peas in a Bucket

METAL ITEMS: Metal Star: Local Craft Store

FABRICS: Local Fabric Store

ADHESIVES: Adhesive Squares by Hermafix; Glue Dots and Glue Lines by Glue Dots International; HeatnBond by Therm O Web

OTHER: Wood Square; Black Embroidery Floss

TOOLS: Sewing Needle; Pencil; Sewing Machine; Iron

INSTRUCTIONS

1. Trim several pictures of your home, or of any favorite things, into small sizes.

2. Tear the top of an 8 ½" x 11" sheet of black cardstock.

3. Attach black cardstock to a 12" x 12" sheet of cardstock in a color of your choice.

4. Adhere photos to black cardstock and right side of colored cardstock using Hermafix squares.

5. Stitch together a quilt block, approximately 5" x 5".

6. Use Glue Lines to attach pieces of fabric and quilt block to top of 12" x 12" sheet.

7. Cover wood square with a piece of fabric and attach button.

8. Use a pencil to write a phrase on muslin (such as "handmade by Kim"). Trace the phrase in black embroidery floss using a primitive backstitch as shown.

9. Follow manufacturer's instructions for HeatnBond on fabric for "Smile"; cut out.

10. Print "Things around the house that make me" on cardstock using David Walker font; add color with red ink.

11. Attach "Smile" button on fabric-covered square and quilt square to top of cardstock with black embroidery floss.

Things around the house that make me smile... When I put this layout together, I had fun thinking about the many things I have in my home that I love. First I thought about my husband, then my two kitties. I thought about all the quilts I've made and the amount of time I spent on them. I thought about simple things that mean nothing to someone else, but mean so much to me. I thought of the gifts my friends and relatives have made just for me. I have "sew" many things that I cherish around the house. I enjoy seeing how my favorites change as my life moves along.

I LOVE THE TIME
WE SPEND TOGETHER

Kim Henkel

My husband and I enjoy spending all of our time together; it is the way it is meant to be as husband and wife. We always seem to enjoy the simple things when we travel, as we love being together wherever we go. We love nature and seeing anything new, even if it is just a blossom.

MATERIALS

RUBBER STAMPS: Alphabet by Hero Arts; Barnes & Noble Clock by Inkadinkado Rubber Stamps

DYE INKPADS: Black and Light Green

PAPERS: Cardstock: Local Craft Store; Patterned Papers by Chatterbox

COMPUTER FONTS: Two Peas in a Bucket

METAL ITEMS: Frame and Photo Corners by Making Memories

RIBBONS: Local Fabric Store

FABRIC: Cotton Muslin: Local Fabric Store; Vintage Wool: Local Antique Store

ADHESIVES: Adhesive Squares by Hermafix; Scrappy Glue by Magic Scraps

OTHER: Star Button; Charm; Antique Buttons; Embroidery Floss; Handmade Papers

TOOLS: Sewing Machine; Embroidery Needle; Button Cover Kit by Dritz

INSTRUCTIONS

1. Cut photos to desired size and attach to a 12" x 12" piece of patterned paper.

2. Cut two different sizes of handmade paper to fill in between photos on top half of page.

3. Use Scrappy Glue to randomly attach metal photo corners to photos.

4. Follow manufacturer's instructions for button kit to cover buttons with cotton muslin.

5. Use alphabet stamps to stamp "TIME" on covered buttons. Sew buttons to wool using embroidery floss as shown.

6. Stamp "I love the" and "we spend together" on cardstock using alphabet rubber stamps; attach to wool with small dots of Scrappy Glue.

7. Use light green ink to stamp clock image on cotton muslin; attach muslin to wool.

8. Create a small pocket for journaling by cutting a strip of muslin approximately 12" x 5". Fold piece of muslin horizontally and machine-stitch both sides; leave a small piece on top of muslin for flap of envelope to fold over. Turn pocket right side out and press down with your fingers. Fold edge of flap under and hand-sew with embroidery floss using a primitive running stitch.

9. Use computer font to print journaling for inside pocket and "Our day in the desert" on tan cardstock.

10. Slip journaling inside handmade pocket. "Our day in the desert" will go on the top of the envelope.

11. Stitch an "X" over the cardstock journaling strip "Our day in the desert" using embroidery floss, as shown.

12. Tie a piece of ribbon around right side of metal frame; use Scrappy Glue to glue frame on top of envelope and three old buttons inside of frame.

13. Attach buttons, charm and beads with embroidery floss.

14. Glue rick rack to top of wool.

15. Tie a piece of ribbon around the middle of the page.

i love
the

TIME

we spend
together

Our day in the desert...

51

I created this layout using photos I took of my son right after he turned 13. I wanted to show the way he looked and what he liked to do, but even more importantly, I wanted to capture his personality and who he really was at that time in his life. I loved the way all the photos turned out, and I think they do show some of his real essence as a person.

CARLENE FEDERER

*C*arlene Federer began scrapbooking almost ten years ago. Her hobby soon grew to include all of the paper arts, and her supply space expanded from a table in her laundry room to a spare bedroom-turned-studio... a wonderful surprise birthday gift from her husband. Carlene's work has appeared in *Creating Keepsakes* and *Legacy* magazines and will also be featured in upcoming issues of several other magazines and idea books. She enjoys the creative process as much as preserving memories, and changes styles to suit her mood, whether it's romantic, vintage, graphic or simple. Because of her eclectic tastes, she has a hard time defining her personal style, but if she had to, she'd call it, "vintage funky." Carlene lives in Tempe, Arizona with her husband and son.

DESTINATION: 13 *Carlene Federer*

TECHNIQUE: *Blender pen transfer and packing tape transfer methods.*

MATERIALS

PAPERS: Cardstock: Local Craft Store

MARKERS: Blender Pen: Local Craft Store

RUB-ONS: "Destination" by Making Memories

METAL ITEMS: Metal Plate by 7gypies; Eyelets and Metal Phrase by Making Memories; Magnetic Words by Magnetic Poetry

ADHESIVES: Mono Permanent Adhesive by Tombow

OTHER: Packing Tape; Measuring Tape; Filmstrip; Dictionary; Foam Core; Elastic; Watch Face by 7gypies

TOOLS: Dymo Labelmaker; Stapler; Bone Folder or Spoon

INSTRUCTIONS

1. Emboss labels for the layout using Dymo Labelmaker.

2. Staple picture on top right and bottom left of page.

3. Adhere filmstrip and Dymo labels to layout as shown.

4. Apply "Destination" rub-on as shown.

MINI BOOKLET:

1. Make mini book out of folded cardstock. Cut out foam core to fit around mini book; add cardstock over top of foam core.

2. Rub on "Destination" on left side of layout. Add photos, filmstrip, Dymo labels and staples to layout.

3. Blender Pen Technique: Mount a toner photocopy face down onto cover of mini book; saturate with blender pen. Use a spoon or bone folder to transfer image to cover of book by rubbing firmly on the back of the photocopy. Pull up corner of copy to make sure transfer is complete; discard copy.

4. Packing Tape Transfer Technique: Stick packing tape to front of toner type photocopy. Use a spoon or bone folder to firmly stick the copy to the tape. Soak the tape in warm water for a few minutes, then gently rub away the copy.

5. Stick the packing tape copy to the metal plate. Add Magnetic Poetry words "summer" and "boy" to metal plate. Add dictionary definition of "thirteen" to metal plate with magnet.

6. Add Making Memories metal phrase, watch face, Dymo label and piece of measuring tape to front of mini book; add metal plate to front of mini book with eyelets.

7. Place two eyelets diagonally across the opening cut in the foam core; thread elastic through eyelets. Add mini book to layout under elastic.

54

LOLA ST. JOHN
Carlene Federer

MATERIALS

DYE INKPADS: Brown: Local Craft Store

PAPERS: Patterned Paper by FoofaLa

PAINTS: Color Wash (Lavender) by 7gypsies

MARKERS: Size .05 Marking Pen: Local Craft Store

RUB-ONS: Simply Stated by Making Memories

TAGS: Punch-Out Tags by FoofaLa

ADHESIVES: Mono Permanent Adhesive by Tombow

OTHER: Vintage Atlas Page; Filmstrip; Rhinestones

INSTRUCTIONS

1. Distress edges of atlas page, tags and photo with color wash and brown ink; layer onto patterned paper.

2. Use rub-on phrases on filmstrip. Adhere small arrow tags to filmstrip and attach filmstrip to page.

3. Layer photo and "wings" over papers at an angle as shown.

4. Use rub-on letters to spell "Lola St. John" on large tag and attach with square rhinestone.

5. Write "circa 1927" on small tag; attach with small rhinestones.

This photo is of one of my "adopted ancestors." I found it in an antique store and had to have it as my own! I just love everything about this picture: the great old car, the woman's outfit and her devil-may-care, flapper attitude! I just know she's going places; so I used vintage atlas paper paired with bright and modern elements, because I'm sure she was a real Modern Millie!

NAUGHTY

Carlene Federer

I took this photo of my little Yorkie, Daisy, after she had been locked outside for being Naughty! She loves to swim in our pool, and we had all been outside swimming, when Daisy decided to make a special trip into the house to go "T-T" on the carpet! I had to admonish her and lock her outside because she was so naughty, but she looked so darn cute, peeking in through the back door, there was no way I could stay mad at her for very long!

MATERIALS

RUBBER STAMPS: "Priceless" Bar Code by River City Rubberworks

PAPERS: Patterned Papers by Making Memories and Jenni Bowlin for Li'l Davis Designs; Cardstock: Local Craft Store

PIGMENT INKPADS: Primrose: Local Craft Store

MARKERS: Size .05 Marking Pen: Local Craft Store

TAGS: Local Craft Store

METAL ITEMS: Brads: Local Craft Store

RIBBONS: Green and Black: Local Craft Store

FABRICS: Printed Twill by 7gypsies

ADHESIVES: Mono Permanent Adhesive by Tombow

OTHER: Tickets; Daisy Die Cut; Glass Letter "d" by Making Memories

INSTRUCTIONS

1. Layer patterned papers onto cardstock as shown. Run "naughty" twill vertically down cardstock; attach with brads.

2. Mount photo onto black cardstock. Tie black ribbon around photo.

3. Wrap green ribbon vertically around black cardstock and tie in a bow as shown.

4. Wrap printed twill horizontally around cardstock and secure with brads.

5. Stamp "priceless" onto tag and hang from brad.

6. Add daisy die cut; adhere the letter "d" in center and attach to top of green ribbon "stem."

7. Write journaling on tag; add tag and tickets.

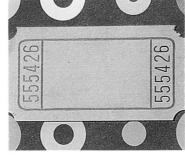

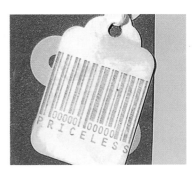

This was such a fun layout to do! I just love these photos of my son right when he turned four.
I used lots of patterned papers and used the number "4" on the layout several times. The
magnet that is attached to the large envelope features different kinds of "4" magnets. The
envelope is slit down the right side and across the bottom and opens like a book, so you can
read the journaling inside.

DANE AT 4
Carlene Federer

MATERIALS

DYE INKPADS: Brown and Light Tan: Local Craft Store

PAPERS: Jenni Bowlin for Li'l Davis Designs; Rusty Pickle; Ledger Paper by Making Memories; Vellum: Local Craft Store

MARKERS: Marking Pen: Local Craft Store

TAGS: Local Craft Store

METAL ITEMS: Hinge and Door Knocker by FoofaLa; Metal Plate by 7gypsies; Typewriter Key by Paper Bliss; "for" Magnet by Magnetic Poetry; "4" Magnet by Running Press; Brads: Local Craft Store

ADHESIVES: Mono Permanent Adhesive by Tombow

OTHER: Stencil by Making Memories; Envelope, Petit Tab and Index Tab by 7gypsies

TOOLS: Sandpaper

INSTRUCTIONS

1. Tear, ink and layer patterned papers. Lightly sand and ink photos; add to layout.

2. Cut large envelope down right side and across the bottom to allow it to open like a book.

3. Add patterned paper to envelope. Attach metal plate with brads; add door knocker, tag and magnets to front of envelope.

4. Print journaling on vellum and mount inside envelope. Add envelope to layout.

5. Add stencil letter "4", hinge and tabs.

FAMILY CIRCLE

Carlene Federer

MATERIALS

PIGMENT INKPADS: Antique Red: Local Craft Store

PAPERS: Rusty Pickle; Circle Mat by K&Company

PAINTS: Red: Local Craft Store

WORDS, LETTERS OR STICKERS: Measuring Tape by Nostalgiques by EK Success

METAL ITEMS: Typewriter Keys by Paper Bliss; Star Brads by Westrim Crafts; Brads: Local Craft Store

FABRICS: Printed Twill by 7gypsies

ADHESIVES: Mono Permanent Adhesive by Tombow

OTHER: Cardboard; Rhinestones; Waxed Linen; Vintage Brass "F"; Watch Parts, Watch Face and Propeller by 7gypsies; Vintage Optometrist's Lens by ARTchix Studio

TOOLS: Sponge Brushes; Petroleum Jelly; Pencil

TECHNIQUE: *Petroleum Jelly Paint Resist Technique*

INSTRUCTIONS

1. Petroleum Jelly Paint Resist Technique: Apply coat of paint over circle mat; let dry. When paint is dry, add a thick coat of petroleum jelly over areas where you don't want a new coat of paint to show through. Paint a contrasting coat of paint over mat. When dry, wipe off petroleum jelly to create a peeling, aged look.

2. Distress cardboard for back by tearing and inking. Lay circle mat over cardboard and lightly trace circles in pencil. This creates a guideline to follow when placing photos and embellishments.

3. Copy small vintage photos onto cardstock. Randomly distress and tear photos. Apply photos and embellishments to cardboard where indicated by traced circles.

4. Back vintage sign piece with patterned paper; use brads to attach sign piece to circle mat.

5. Erase any visible pencil marks from cardboard; adhere circle mat to cardboard.

6. Punch holes through mat and cardboard. Tie twine onto optometrist's lens; feed other end through punched hole. Knot printed twill through holes to create a hanger. Tuck optometrist's lens behind sign piece.

7. Use typewriter keys to spell "family circle" on circle mat.

Many of the vintage photos I've gotten from my dad and Aunt Bernice are much smaller than the photographs we're used to today. I had a lot of them, but they are really hard to showcase on a regular-sized layout, so I wasn't sure what to do with them. Then I found this great circle mat, and viola! I had a perfect solution for all those little photos! I had so much fun placing the photos and accents. I'd found a great vintage sign piece of the letter "F" for our last name, "Federer," and added it to the middle of the mat to symbolize our family. I also had a vintage optometrist's lens and decided to add it behind the "F" so the photos could be viewed closer. This layout was a lot of fun to do, and I'm always happy when I can get my photos out of storage and displayed where they can be seen and enjoyed.

COME OUT AND PLAY

Carlene Federer

MATERIALS

PIGMENT INKPADS: Browns and Light Tan: Local Craft Store

PAPERS: Citrus Stripe and Confused by BasicGrey

PAINTS: Color Wash (Pastel Pink) by 7gypsies

WORDS, LETTERS OR STICKERS: Measuring Tape by Nostalgiques by EK Success

RUB-ONS: Simply Stated by Making Memories

METAL ITEMS: Brads by Bazzill Basics

RIBBONS: Local Craft Store

ADHESIVES: Mono Permanent Adhesive by Tombow

OTHER: Rounderz by Junkitz

INSTRUCTIONS

1. Tear patterned papers, ink edges and adhere to cardstock.

2. Distress edges of photo with ink and color wash.

3. Tie small ribbons to photo. Add larger ribbon across bottom of photo with brads; add to layout.

4. Apply rub-on words "come out and play, have fun".

5. Use Rounderz as shown. Add ribbon along left side and bottom of layout.

6. Add measuring tape sticker to finish.

I love this picture of my Aunt Bernice and a friend taken in the yard of my grandparents' home. To anyone who has ever lived there, the Wyoming prairie is immediately recognizable; there is nothing as far as the eye can see! In those days, a lot of pictures were taken featuring the family car in the background. I'm glad that was the custom, because it's so fun today seeing those old cars in photos. Because of this, I've made it a practice to take some pictures with our family cars in the background. Maybe years from now, someone will enjoy seeing our "old-fashioned" cars! I also enjoy seeing how many of my old family photos have animals in them: dogs, cats, sheep, cows and horses. On a ranch, animals were a crucial part of my family's everyday lives and how they made their living.

ALL TRUE TALES OF EDNA & HER CHICKENS

Carlene Federer

MATERIALS

RUBBER STAMPS: Fork by Wordsworth

PIGMENT INKPADS: Clear: Local Craft Store

DYE INKPADS: Browns and Light Tan: Local Craft Store

PAPERS: Anna Griffin; K&Company; Karen Foster Designs; Vellum by Daisy D's

RUB-ONS: Letters by Autumn Leaves

TAGS: 7gypsies

TRANSPARENCIES: Local Office Supply

RIBBONS: Black and White Checkered: Local Craft Store

ADHESIVES: Mono Permanent Adhesive by Tombow

OTHER: Feathers; Vintage Labels by FoofaLa; Envelope by Memory Lane; Scrapbook Tacks by Chatterbox

INSTRUCTIONS

1. Print fried chicken recipe on transparency; let dry. Print journaling on vellum; attach to tags with ribbon.

2. Mount blue paper onto red striped paper using scrapbook tacks.

3. Attach transparency to patterned papers.

4. Distress edges of photo and adhere to layout.

5. Cut out chickens from patterned paper. Add torn patterned paper to part of envelope; attach envelope and chickens to page.

6. Apply rub-on letters to labels to create title.

7. Use pigment ink to stamp fork on envelope and along bottom of patterned paper.

Grandma's chickens were almost like pets and would come running every time Grandma came outside! She always let me help her feed them and gather the eggs... some of my favorite childhood memories.

GREAT DANES
Carlene Federer

MATERIALS

RUBBER STAMPS: Date Stamp by Postmodern Design

PIGMENT INKPADS: ColorBox by Clearsnap

DYE INKPADS: Light Tan: Local Craft Store

PAPERS: K&Company; Rusty Pickle; Bravissimo! Paper

WORDS, LETTERS OR STICKERS: Measuring Tape by Nostalgiques by EK Success

MESH: Black Mesh by Magic Mesh

METAL ITEMS: Brads by Gary M. Burlin & Company

ADHESIVES: Mono Permanent Adhesive by Tombow

OTHER: Dictionary; Vintage Postcard; Stencil Letter; Copper Coin Letters; Ticket; Alligator Clip, Photo Turn and Index Tab by 7gypsies

INSTRUCTIONS

1. Tear, ink and layer patterned papers.

2. Add mesh to upper right-hand corner.

3. Cover stencil letter "D" with patterned paper, measuring tape sticker and dictionary definition; add to layout with clip.

4. Ink edges of vintage postcard and photo. Ink dictionary definition for Great Dane; add to photo and adhere to layout.

5. Add photo turn with brads; add coin letters to spell "Dane" inside tab.

6. Add measuring tape sticker on left side of layout; add photo turn.

7. Distress and fold ticket in half; staple to photo.

8. Randomly stamp layout.

My cousin, who lives in Oklahoma, was helping some people clean out an old abandoned house. They threw out tons of garbage and debris. Someone was getting ready to throw out a big box of papers, when my cousin stopped them and told them she wanted to send it to her cousin in Arizona. They said, "Why would she want this, it's just a box of garbage!" She replied, "Believe me, she'll want it." You know the old saying "One man's junk is another man's treasure?" That was certainly true in this case! In the box were old calendars, magazines, postcards, letters, etc., truly a treasure for me! Included was an old postcard with Great Dane dogs on it. My son's name is Dane, so I knew I had to do a layout with the postcard and a photo of him. I added dictionary definitions for "Great Dane" and a stencil letter "D" for Dane. This layout was so much fun for me!

I don't know very much about my Great Aunt Rose's life - just a few bare facts. She was my grandfather's sister. Her husband abandoned her and their three little girls, and she and the girls ran a homestead on the Wyoming prairie by themselves for many years. Her life must have been really tough. I just had to use the feathers on this layout to mimic the ones on her fabulous hat, and I also used a lot of "flight" imagery, because I imagined there were a lot of times she wished she were free of all her chores and responsibilities.

GREAT AUNT ROSE

Carlene Federer

MATERIALS

RUBBER STAMPS: Hero Arts; Inkadinkado Rubber Stamps

PIGMENT INKPADS: Sepia, Brown and Light Tan

PAPERS: 7gypsies; Anna Griffin

WORDS, LETTERS OR STICKERS: Postage Sticker by Nostalgiques by EK Success

RUB-ONS: Letters by Making Memories

TAGS: Vellum Tags by Making Memories; Jewelry Tags: Local Craft Store

TRANSPARENCIES: Librarie Layer by 7gypsies

METAL ITEMS: Small Silver Frame by 7gypsies

ADHESIVES: Mod Podge by Plaid; Mono Permanent Adhesive by Tombow

OTHER: Vintage Album Page; Vintage Dictionary Paper; Angel Charm; Photo Corners; Rhinestones; Feathers; Silver Arrow; Paper Rose by The Card Connection

INSTRUCTIONS

1. Tear and ink edges of patterned papers; layer onto background paper.

2. Tear and ink edges of transparency; adhere over patterned papers.

3. Mount photo on cardstock; ink edges. Add photo corners and adhere to layout.

4. Glue angel charm onto jewelry tag. Tie jewelry tag to small silver frame. Glue frame to photo; add paper rose to frame.

5. Back vellum tag with vintage dictionary paper; apply rub-on letter "R" to tag. Adhere tag to layout.

6. Stamp wings on either side of vellum tag. Glue rhinestone to jewelry tag and add to vellum tag.

7. Cut words "oh that I had wings like a dove" from Librarie Layer; glue onto jewelry tags. Tie tags around silver arrow; adhere arrow to layout.

8. Back vintage photo frame with patterned paper. Use rub-on letters to spell "Great Aunt Rose" on frame and patterned paper; add to layout.

9. Tuck feather spray behind photo; add stamp to upper left corner.

10. Randomly use inkpads on layout for distressed finish.

ROSE'S GIRLS
Carlene Federer

This photo is of my Great

Aunt Rose's three little girls.

They are all so adorable

with their curls and bows!

I used much of the same

materials on this layout as I

did on the one about Great

Aunt Rose in order to link

them together.

MATERIALS

RUBBER STAMPS: Hero Arts; Inkadin-kado Rubber Stamps

PIGMENT INKPADS: Sepia, Brown and Light Tan: Local Craft Store

PAPERS: Toile, Striped and Floral Patterned Papers by Anna Griffin

WORDS, LETTERS OR STICKERS: Postcard by 7gypsies; Label Stickers: Local Craft Store

RUB-ONS: Simply Stated by Making Memories

TAGS: Vellum Tags by Making Memories; Jewelry Tags: Local Craft Store

TRANSPARENCIES: Local Office Supply

METAL ITEMS: Silver Bar by Embellish-It; Small Silver Frame by 7gypsies

ADHESIVES: Mod Podge by Plaid; Mono Permanent Adhesive by Tombow; Double-Stick Scotch Tape by 3M

OTHER: Vintage Seed Catalog Page; Vintage Album Page; Photo Corners; Rhinestones; Paper Roses by The Card Connection

INSTRUCTIONS

1. Tear edges of striped and floral papers; layer over toile paper. Adhere to scrapbook page.

2. Print vintage seed catalog page onto transparency; tape to background.

3. Distress-ink edges of photo; double-mat and add photo corners.

4. Use rub-on letters to spell "Rose's Girls" onto patterned paper; adhere to back of vintage photo album page and adhere to layout.

5. Stamp rose image onto vellum tag; adhere to layout. Stamp wings on either side of vellum tag.

6. Glue paper roses onto jewelry tags; adhere behind vellum tag.

7. Add stickers to corners of layout; add silver bar above vellum tag.

8. Glue three rhinestones to small piece of scrap paper; glue silver frame over paper. Adhere to layout.

9. Randomly run ink over layout for distressed finish.

JEN
Carlene Federer

MATERIALS

RUBBER STAMPS: "Priceless" Bar Code by River City Rubberworks

PIGMENT INKPADS: Primrose: Local Craft Store

DYE INKPADS: Browns and Light Tan: Local Craft Store

PAPERS: Pink Floral Pattern by Jenni Bowlin for Li'l Davis Designs; Phont, Phlordilee and Phresh Monograms by BasicGrey; Vellum: Local Craft Store

PAINTS: Color Wash (Pastel Pink) by 7gypsies

TAGS: Local Craft Store

METAL ITEMS: Brads by Bazzill Basics

RIBBONS: Ribbons and Rick Rack: Local Craft or Fabric Store

ADHESIVES: Mono Permanent Adhesive by Tombow

OTHER: Flower Charm; Photo Corners by Canson

INSTRUCTIONS

1. Layer vellum over Jenni Bowlin pink floral-patterned paper. Add BasicGrey patterned paper down right-hand side and left corner of layout.

2. Distress edges of photo with pastel pink color wash and mat on patterned paper; add photo corners as shown.

3. Stamp "priceless" on tag; string onto rick rack and attach using brads.

4. Punch out BasicGrey monograms to spell "Jen"; add flower charm to center of the dot above "J".

This photo of my friend's daughter really captures her personality. I wanted to use lots of bright patterned papers for this photo, but the colors of her dress and the flowers clashed with what I wanted to do. So I converted the picture to black and white, which I think really makes the photo pop out against all the color.

THE MEASURE OF A LIFE

Carlene Federer

This layout is a kind of tribute to my Grandmother Edna. She was such an extraordinary person, and lived through so much in her life without ever losing her sense of humor, her faith, or her love of family. Sadly, I have very few photos of her, but I scanned and framed the ones I did have and ran them down the left-hand side of the layout to show her at different times of her life.

MATERIALS

PAPERS: Floral by Anna Griffin; Vellum by The Paper Company; Cardstock: Local Craft Store

WORDS, LETTERS OR STICKERS: Measuring Tape Stickers by Nostalgiques by EK Success and Marcella by Kay; Typewriter Keys by Nostalgiques by EK Success; Blossoms by Making Memories

METAL ITEMS: Brads by Bazzill Basics and Coffee Break Designs; Small Gold Frames, Charms and Gold Photo Corners: Local Craft Store

RIBBONS: Local Craft Store

ADHESIVES: Mono Permanent Adhesive by Tombow

OTHER: Tickets; Coin Holder by 7gypsies; Watch Face by Li'l Davis Designs

TOOLS: Sandpaper

INSTRUCTIONS

1. Lightly sand patterned paper. Cut one-third of the way across; mount to cardstock with "stripes" of cardstock showing.

2. Type journaling on vellum; adhere to layout.

3. Add measuring tape stickers along side, middle and bottom of page as shown.

4. With typewriter key stickers, spell "The measure of a life" on tickets. Add tickets to top of layout; add ribbon on top of tickets.

5. Frame small photos in gold frames. Create a mini collage on left side of layout with frames, charms and blossoms.

6. Add large watch face to lower right corner of layout, and metal photo corners on top.

7. Add rhinestones for final embellishment.

THE MEASURE OF A LIFE

The person I have admired most in my life has been my late grandmother, Edna Mae Parker Federer. She and my Grandfather homesteaded on the Wyoming prairie when she was only 16, living a life that was so hard we can only imagine it today. She lived through three wars and the Great Depression. She had eight children, and buried three; her first son, a newborn baby who died from SIDS, another son who lost his life in battle during WWII, and a son that lost a battle with cancer in his 60's. During World War II three of her four sons were over-seas, fighting for our country. An entire book could be written of the hardships and suffering she went through in her lifetime.

Yet none of the things that happened to her could ever keep her down. She had a wonderful sense of humor, and loved to laugh. When her kids were growing up, they always knew they could get out of trouble if they could make their "ma" laugh, and they usually could. She missed church only when illness or blizzard kept her away. She volunteered at her church, and other clubs in town. She was an excellent cook, especially known for her noodles, breads, pies and fried chicken, and loved to feed anyone she could. She was also famous for her beautiful quilts, pieced and quilted by hand, using only clothes and linens that couldn't be mended anymore. Each of her children, grandchildren and great-grandchildren have at least one of her handmade quilts. She donated a quilt to one of her charities every year. The charity always sold every raffle ticket they had, because everyone wanted to win one of Edna's quilts.

Her large vegetable garden took up a lot of her time, but she always had African Violets on her windowsills, and hollyhocks growing in the yard.

I never heard her raise her voice, or speak in anger. She had many grand and great-grandchildren, and every one of us knew we were special to Grandma.

Although she has been gone for over 20 years, her children, grandchildren, great grandchildren, friends and neighbors still speak of her often, and with great affection.

I guess I would say the biggest attribute I learned from my Grandma is to always keep a positive attitude. Despite all the trials she went through, she never lost her huge enjoyment of life. Her faith, love of family, hard work, service to others, and sense of humor made her a truly remarkable person. I can only hope to try to emulate the worthwhile way she lived her life.

PAPILLON
Carlene Federer

MATERIALS

PAPERS: Amber Tiles and Vine by Creative Imaginations

RUB-ONS: Letters (Playbill Bark) by Heidi Swapp

TRANSPARENCIES: Papillon by ARTchix Studio

METAL ITEMS: Plain Brads by Karen Foster Design; Antique Brads by Making Memories; T-pins: Local Craft Store

FIBERS: Gold: Local Craft Store

ADHESIVES: Mono Permanent Adhesive by Tombow

INSTRUCTIONS

1. Tie fiber around photo; secure fiber with T-pin. Adhere to patterned paper with brad.

2   Wrap long butterfly transparency with fiber as shown, running the fiber through the brads while attaching to patterned paper.

3. Attach another small piece of the butterfly transparency to the lower right side of layout using T-pins. Add fiber around one pin.

4. Apply rub-on letters to spell "Papillon" (French for butterfly).

5. Add a small butterfly transparency to the little girl's hair.

This is another layout done with an "instant ancestor" that I saw at a flea market. I had no immediate plans for this photo, but kept it out on my desk so that I could admire it. A few days later, I got an awesome butterfly transparency sheet that I wanted to use… serendipity! I'd use the transparency on a layout with the little girl's photo. I wove the fiber pieces around the brads to create a kind of "cocoon" effect over the butterfly transparencies, and for a whimsical touch, I added a tiny butterfly to the little girl's hair!

BaD Photo

GOOD FRIEND

Girlfriends

GIRLS ROCK!

I KNOW, I KNOW, THIS PICTURE OF ME & MY FRIEND JACKIE IS JUST AWFUL! (WE'RE BOTH MUCH, MUCH CUTER IN REAL LIFE, HONEST!) THE LIGHTING IS ALL WRONG THE BACK GROUND IS DISTRACTING, WE'RE NOT CENTERED OR IN FOCUS... THE WIND IS BLOWING 90 MILES AN HOUR & IT'S FREEZING! BUT... THIS IS THE ONLY PHOTO OF US THAT CAME OUT WHEN I DEVELOPED MY FILM. MY FIRST THOUGHT WAS TO TOSS IT IN THE BOX WITH ALL THE OTHER PHOTOS THAT DIDN'T TURN OUT, BUT THEN I THOUGHT, TO HECK WITH IT! YEAH, IT'S A REALLY BAD SHOT, BUT JACKIE LIVES IN WYOMING, & I'M IN ARIZONA & I HARDLY EVER EVER GET TO SEE HER SO I'M USING IT ANYWAY! HEY, IT'S THE MEMORY THAT COUNTS, RIGHT?

BAD PHOTO/GOOD FRIEND
Carlene Federer

MATERIALS

PAPERS: Cardstock: Local Craft Store

PAINT: Cornflower by Making Memories

MARKERS: Size .08 Marking Pen (Black)

RUB-ONS: Letters (Black) and Large Harlequin by Distressed Effects by My Mind's Eye; Letters (Aloha Pink) by Rusty Pickle; Diamond Drama (Small and Medium Harlequins, Flourish and Box) by Heidi Swapp; Blue Star, Girls Rock! and Girlfriends by Making Memories

ADHESIVES: Mono Permanent Adhesive by Tombow

OTHER: Rhinestones; Pink Decorative Tape and Ghost Frame by Heidi Swapp; Paper Flowers by Prima by Martin/F. Weber Co.

INSTRUCTIONS

1. Paint edges of cardstock with Cornflower paint; let dry.
2. Mount photo to ghost frame; rub on "Bad Photo" and "Girlfriends" and attach to layout.
3. Apply a pattern of large and small harlequin rub-ons to cardstock.
4. Add decorative tape along right-hand side of page; add journaling.
5. Rub on "Good Friend", "Girls Rock!" and blue star.
6. Finish with rhinestones and flowers.

I went crazy with the harlequin rub-ons in this layout! I used a combination of sizes and styles, all tied together with pink and blue accents.

I love this picture my son took... this little wildflower was all by itself in the middle of nowhere. The quote and the photo just seem made for each other!

WILDFLOWER

Carlene Federer

MATERIALS

PIGMENT INKPADS: Medium Brown: Local Craft Store

PAPERS: Spring Plaid by Junkitz

RUB-ONS: Pieces of Me (Orange) by KI Memories; Typewriter (Brown): Local Craft Store

METAL ITEMS: Paper Clips by Nostalgiques by EK Success; Metal Label Holder: Local Craft Store

ADHESIVES: Mono Permanent Adhesive by Tombow

OTHER: Artisan Label by Making Memories; Tape (Endless Summer) by Heidi Swapp; Vintage Dictionary Paper

INSTRUCTIONS

1. Using a ruler as a guide, tear photo. Ink edges and mount to patterned paper.

2. Use a variety of rub-on letters in a "ransom" style to add quote to top of layout and word to bottom of layout.

3. Tear definitions from vintage dictionaries. Mount "flower" definition on top of "wild" definition; frame "flower" with label holder.

4. Mount definitions to Artisan Label; add to layout.

5. Run tape along bottom of layout to frame title, and diagonally across top left-hand corner of photo.

6. Add paper clip to finish.

These photos were taken one spring when my dad came down from Wyoming to visit. We were all dressed up to go somewhere, so what better time to take photos? Most of the "generational" layouts I've seen are with just the men, or just the women in a family, but since that photo is never going to happen in my family, I decided to make my own version of the "generational" layout!

3 GENERATIONS

Carlene Federer

MATERIALS

PAPERS: Phresh & Phunky Phern by BasicGrey

MARKERS: Size .05 Marking Pen (Pink): Local Craft Store

RUB-ONS: Aloha Black by Rusty Pickle

ADHESIVES: Mono Permanent Adhesive by Tombow

PAINTS: Color Wash (Pastel Pink) by 7gypsies

OTHER: Vintage Number "3"; Dice; Measuring Tape; Watch Face and Parts by 7gypsies; Filmstrip by Karen Foster Design

TOOLS: Dymo Labelmaker; Stapler

INSTRUCTIONS

1. Print color photo in black and white; distress edges with Color Wash. Add to patterned paper.

2. Cut photos to fit in filmstrip; add to bottom of layout.

3. Use rub-on letters to spell your family name under main photo.

4. Add vintage "3" to right side of layout. Emboss "generations" with label maker and adhere to page under "3".

5. Add dice, watch face and watch parts.

6. Staple measuring tape to left side of layout. Write in names and date with marking pen.

2 CHERISH

Carlene Federer

This is a photo of my great aunt and uncle on their wedding day. I really like it because they look a little less stiff than a lot of the vintage wedding photos I've seen, and they seem to be genuinely happy together. As I was looking through my stash of "stuff" for inspiration for my scrapbook layouts, as I often do, I found a vintage sign piece of the number "2." That became my jumping off point for the layout. I gathered other "2s" to use to symbolize their togetherness, and used rub-on words to create a "loving" layout.

MATERIALS

RUBBER STAMPS: Sponge by Plaid

PIGMENT INKPADS: Browns and Light Tan: Local Craft Store

PAPERS: Motifica, Chalk Motif and Circus Stripe by BasicGrey

PAINTS: Color Wash (Lavender) by 7gypsies

WORDS, LETTERS OR STICKERS: "2" Sticker by BasicGrey

RUB-ONS: Simply Stated (White) by Making Memories

TAGS: Jewelry Tag: Local Craft Store

TRANSPARENCIES: Autumn Leaves

METAL ITEMS: Heart Brad, Gold Leaf Corners and Small Metal "2" by ARTchix Studio; Brads by Bazzill Basics; Large Brass "2" and Small Gold Frame: Local Craft Store

FIBERS: Bazzill Basics

RIBBONS: Local Craft Store

ADHESIVES: Mono Permanent Adhesive by Tombow

OTHER: Lace and Rhinestones: Local Craft Store

TOOLS: Tag Punch by Marvy Uchida

INSTRUCTIONS

1. Punch tags from patterned paper.
2. Distress cardstock, patterned paper, tags and photo with lavender color wash and pigment inks.
3. Stamp patterned paper with sponge image.
4. Mount patterned paper on cardstock; add transparency.
5. Add accents to tags; add tags to layout.
6. Write words on ribbon with rub-ons; add across bottom of layout with brads.
7. Attach ribbon on right-hand side of page with brads.
8. Glue on rhinestones to finish.

SWING!

Carlene Federer

MATERIALS

DYE INKPADS: Browns: Local Craft Store

PAPERS: Phresh & Phunky, Phoilage, Phunny, Phont and Phlordilee by BasicGrey

RUB-ONS: Montage and Punctuate by Autumn Leaves; Simply Stated by Making Memories

TAGS: Phresh Tags by BasicGrey

METAL ITEMS: Conchos by Scrapworks; Brads: Local Craft Store

RIBBONS: Ribbons and Rick Rack: Local Craft Store

FABRICS: Printed Twill by 7gypsies

ADHESIVES: Mono Permanent Adhesive by Tombow

OTHER: Rhinestones; Tickets by Memory Lane; Silk Flowers by Making Memories

INSTRUCTIONS

1. Layer patterned papers; ink edges of photos. Adhere photos to page as shown.

2. Run ribbon along left side and top; run printed twill along bottom by adhering with conchos and brads.

3. Apply rub-on letters to BasicGrey tags along with monogram "S" to spell "Swing."

4. "Hang" tags and monogram from ribbon; add rub-on exclamation point.

5. Glue rhinestones to centers of double-layered silk flowers and adhere to page.

6. Apply Simply Stated rub-on word "happiness" across torn and inked tickets.

These two photos speak volumes about the happy days of childhood. My friend's daughters look so content and carefree, just as kids should be! I wanted to do a scrapbook page that would be just as light and fun as the photos! I set about to accomplish this by placing the title "Swing!" across the top of the layout on ribbon, using a rub-on word "happy" and adding lots of flowers!

CUPPY CAKE

Carlene Federer

MATERIALS

RUBBER STAMPS: "Priceless" Bar Code by River City Rubberworks

PIGMENT INKPADS: Cyan Blue: Local Craft Store

DYE INKPADS: Brown: Local Craft Store

PAPERS: Aged & Confused Line and Gumballs by BasicGrey; Sweetie Line by SEI; Endearments and Baby Doll by Rusty Pickle

RUB-ONS: Simply Stated by Making Memories; Letters, Stitches and Punctuate by Autumn Leaves; Stamped, Typewriter Rub-Ons by Montreal

TAGS: Local Office Supply

METAL ITEMS: Green Clip: Local Craft Store or Office Supply

ADHESIVES: Mono Permanent Adhesive by Tombow

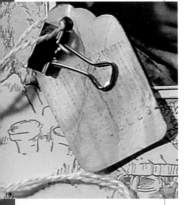

INSTRUCTIONS

1. Layer patterned papers and use rub-on stitches to "sew" the papers together.

2. Mat photo on cardstock; ink edges and adhere to page.

3. Cut out words from Endearments paper to make words of favorite song, nursery rhyme and nicknames; also, use rub-on letters on cardstock and cut out to make words. Rub brown ink around edges of words to age and add to page.

4. Add rub-on exclamation point and quotation marks to page.

5. Stamp "Priceless" to tag and attach to photo with metal clip.

I LOVE this photo of my son, Dane, taken when he was between two and three years old. He has the sweetest little expression on his face, and I love the way he's holding his chubby little hands together. Whenever I looked at this photo, it would remind me of the "Cuppy Cake" song I used to sing to him back then. It's such a cute and silly little song, and I wanted to do a layout with that photo and the words to the song. I cut some of the words out of patterned paper, and used rub-on letters to make the rest. I also added the phrase "sweet pea" to the side of the photo, because that was one of my nicknames for him. Since that memory and photo are truly priceless to me, I stamped a "Priceless" bar code on a tag and added it to the layout.

10 RANDOM FACTS ABOUT ME

Carlene Federer

I saw a challenge on a scrapbooking website to do an "All About Me" layout, and thought it would be fun to try. This is the result of that challenge, and it was very enjoyable to do! Each mini file folder contains one "random fact about me."

MATERIALS

RUBBER STAMPS: "Fact File" by Post-modern Design

PIGMENT INKPADS: Primrose: Local Craft Store

PAPERS: Patterned Papers by Basic-Grey

MARKERS: Marking Pen (Pink): Local Craft Store

RUB-ONS: Letters and Numbers by Autumn Leaves; Pink "ME" by Creative Imaginations

TAGS: Profile Tag by 7gypsies

TRANSPARENCIES: Creative Imaginations

ADHESIVES: Mono Permanent Adhesive by Tombow

OTHER: Plain Mini File Folders by DMD Industries; Printed Mini File Folders by Nostalgiques by EK Success; Manila Envelope

INSTRUCTIONS

1. Mount transparency over patterned paper.

2. Use rub-ons to number file folders 1 thru 10.

3. Journal on inside of folders; adhere to layout.

4. Fill out 7gypsies Profile Tag; add mini photo and adhere to envelope.

5. Stamp "Fact File" on manila envelope. Use rub-ons to spell "10 Random Facts About Me!"

6. Add the stamped envelope to background.

1 -215

I HATE CLUTTER,
2

I LOATHE
3

4

I THINK MY
5

6

BEWITCHED IS
7

8

9

10!

FACT FILE
10 RANDOM FACTS ABOUT ME!

PROFILE •
NAME CARLENE
ALIAS MOM & HONEY WOULD YOU...

ENDEARING QUALITIES
KIND TO ANIMALS,
GOOD COOK,
PUNCTUAL
ANNOYING TRAITS
NO SENSE OF DIRECTION

THIS TAG IS NOT TRANSFERABLE TO ANYONE ELSE. YOU'RE ONE-OF-A-KIND ANYWAY.

PERSONALITY PLUS
DATE OF ISSUE 04/05   ISSUED BY MOI!

RECYCLED PAPER,
MINIMUM 20% POST-CONSUMER
FIBER CONTENT.
Columbian® - 55 Clasp (6 x 9)

TRADITIONAL BAGELS

Carlene Federer

MATERIALS

PIGMENT INKPADS: Tan: Local Craft Store

PAPERS: Sentimental Multi Dots and Sentimental Harlequin Fawn by Scenic Route Paper Company

MARKERS: Marking Pen (Brown): Local Craft Store

RUB-ONS: Pieces of Me (Orange) by KI Memories; Typewriter (Brown) by Autumn Leaves

TAGS: Local Craft Store

METAL ITEMS: Large Brad by Karen Foster Design; Hippie Chick Jeweled Brads by SEI

FIBERS: Local Craft Store

RIBBONS: Local Craft Store

SILK FLOWERS: Local Craft Store

ADHESIVES: Mono Permanent Adhesive by Tombow

OTHER: Rhinestones

INSTRUCTIONS

1. Tear edges of photo. Distress edges of photo, patterned papers and tags.

2. Mount photo to polka dot paper; mount to harlequin paper.

3. Write journaling on tag; add small pieces of photos and journaling on the other tag. Attach tags to layout using jeweled brads.

4. Mount large brad between tags; run ribbon and fibers from tag to tag.

5. Add silk flowers; add rhinestones to center of flowers.

I have a group of friends who all met when our kids started kindergarten. We were room mothers and together served on the PTA and volunteered at school parties and at carnivals. Over the years, we developed many traditions. One that we continue to observe is getting together for bagels after we get our kids off for the very first day of school. It's a great way to catch up and reconnect after our busy summers. I wanted to do a layout to celebrate this fun time.

STEP
into

tHe, CuT & DriED
hAS No PlacE In... LiQuiD

STEP INTO LIQUID
Carlene Federer

MATERIALS

PAPERS: The Paper Loft

PAINTS: Color Wash (Lavender) by 7gypsies

RUB-ONS: Letters (Black) by Making Memories; Letters (White) by Autumn Leaves

TAGS: 7gypsies

TRANSPARENCIES: Local Office Supply

METAL ITEMS: Photo Corners, Brads and Shell Charms: Local Craft Store

ADHESIVES: Mono Permanent Adhesive by Tombow

OTHER: Twine

TECHNIQUE: Printing on transparencies

INSTRUCTIONS

1. Copy photo onto transparency in black and white. Copy on another transparency in color; let dry completely.

2. Apply color wash to tags; let dry and add rub-on letters in black.

3. Apply white rub-on letters for title to patterned paper as shown.

4. Cut transparencies the same size as photo. Stagger black and white transparency, color transparency and color photo across patterned paper. Attach them with metal photo corners.

5. Add brads to left side of layout; string with twine. String shell charms onto tags with twine. Add tags to layout.

My husband, son and I are all big fans of the ocean. We spend almost two weeks on a beach vacation every summer. I had taken this photo of my son two or three years ago, and though I loved the photo, I hadn't found the right way to do a layout with it, I really wanted it to be special. Last summer the three of us saw a documentary called "Step into Liquid," all about the ocean and the people who love it. Needless to say, it was a favorite for all of us. I loved the title of the documentary, and also what one of the people who was interviewed said, which was, "The cut and dried has no place in liquid." I knew right away I'd found the format for the photo of my son. I used the title of the documentary and the quote on my layout. I really like how this turned out - kind of dreamy and surreal, like the ocean itself.

ANNIVERSARY
Carlene Federer

MATERIALS

PIGMENT INKPADS: Brown and Light Tan: Local Craft Store

PAPERS: Making Memories

WORDS, LETTERS OR STICKERS: Defined Stickers by Making Memories; Flower Stickers by Nostalgiques

TAGS: Local Craft Store

METAL ITEMS: Arrow Charm, Brads, Typewriter Key, Calendar, Clock and Hands: Local Craft Store

RIBBONS: Local Craft Store

SILK FLOWERS: Blossoms by Making Memories

ADHESIVES: Mod Podge by Plaid; Mono Permanent Adhesive by Tombow

OTHER: Rhinestones; Tickets

TOOLS: Sandpaper

Greg and I have always had kind of "unusual" luck, so I guess it works for us that I got this beautiful diamond for our 13th wedding anniversary...I (of course) kept my wedding band, which I wouldn't trade for anything, but I sure felt "lucky" to get this gorgeous new diamond for my engagement ring! As if the new "sparkler" weren't enough, Greg also got me two of my other favorite things...Godiva Chocolates and, pink roses!!

INSTRUCTIONS

1. Lightly sand and tear and the patterned papers, tickets and tags. Distress with inks.

2. Layer patterned paper, cardstock and photos.

3. Add patterned paper, Defined Stickers and ribbons to tags; add tags to layout.

4. Add tickets (with stickers "13") on left-hand side of layout; adhere blossoms.

5. Create word "anniversary" with stickers; adhere calendar sticker, flower sticker, blossoms and tickets to layout as shown.

6. Add rhinestones to centers of blossoms.

I found this photograph in an antiques shop in Colorado. I instantly fell in love with these two girls. They look so happy! I wonder who they were and what became of them. I scanned this photograph into my computer and it is now the wallpaper on my desktop.

*R*oben-Marie Smith is a mixed media artist, instructor and designer. Her work has been published in *Artists Creating With Photos, Creating Vintage Cards, Vintage Collage for Scrapbooking* and numerous magazines. She also shares her talents through teaching at various venues around the country, including national art gatherings. Her love for teaching is evident in her style and presentation - a patient and caring approach. Students are thrilled when they leave her classes inspired and especially gratified to have successfully completed a project. Roben-Marie also owns Paperbag Studios, which offers a full line of rubber art stamps. Her creative interests include designing rubber stamps, mixed media collage and book arts. She resides in Port Orange, Florida with her husband of 16 years, Bobby.

JOYFUL *Roben-Marie Smith*

MATERIALS

PAPERS: Brown Cardstock: Local Craft Store; Rivoli Paper by 7gypsies; Red Paper by BasicGrey

PAINTS: Black and White Acrylic Paints: Local Craft Store

RUB-ONS: Making Memories

METAL ITEMS: Red Staples by Making Memories

RIBBONS: Local Craft Store

ADHESIVES: Glue Stick; Glue Dots by Glue Dots International

OTHER: Old Buttons; Red Thread; Writing Paper from Old Book; Corrugated Paper; Old Envelope; Masking Tape; "J" Stencil by Autumn Leaves; Stitched Piece by Li'l Davis Designs

TOOLS: Small Bristle Paint Brush

INSTRUCTIONS

1. Using black acrylic paint, imprint scrapbook paper with the pattern on the corrugated paper, using corrugated paper like a stamp, as shown.

2. Adhere old envelope scrap to middle of page and then glue black and white Making Memories paper to bottom portion of page.

3. Glue old writing paper scrap to top middle of page.

4. Dry brush* white acrylic paint to "J" letter stencil and adhere red BasicGrey paper to the back to show through. Glue stencil to page.

5. Adhere buttons to page with Glue Dots.

6. Add a piece of masking tape to top right of Making Memories paper and staple using red staples.

7. Tie red thread into the holes in the stitched piece and tie red ribbon at each end. Adhere stitched piece to page and pull thread to the sides of page and secure to the back with masking tape.

8. Apply rub-on word to stitched piece.

Dry brush: A technique that uses very little paint on a dry bristle brush to only partially cover area to be painted.

HAPPINESS

Roben-Marie Smith

My niece, Charlie, spent some time with us over the Christmas holidays. Try as I may, I could not get her to smile for the camera. I kept following her around, but she insisted on remaining serious. At that time, Charlie did not say much, and when she did speak, she said only what was needed to get her point across. I kept snapping photos and after a few days, I only ended up with three usable ones. I finally got her to smile in one of them!

MATERIALS

DYE INKPADS: Ginger: Local Craft Store

PAPERS: Printed Paper by 7gypsies; Cardstock from Local Craft Store

PAINTS: White Acrylic Local Craft Store

WORDS, LETTERS OR STICKERS: Bubble Letter by Li'l Davis Designs; Defined Words by Making Memories

RUB-ONS: Making Memories

METAL ITEMS: Copper Metal Frame, Safety Pins and Copper Metal Charm by Li'l Davis Designs; Black Mini Brads: Local Craft Store

RIBBONS: Local Craft Store

FABRICS: Mesh Fabric: Local Craft Store

ADHESIVES: Glue Stick; Glue Dots by Glue Dots International

OTHER: Twine; Silk Flowers; Velvet Leaves by ARTchix Studio

TOOLS: Silk Sponge; Small Bristle Paint Brush

INSTRUCTIONS

1. Tear and glue Defined Words and printed paper to page as shown.

2. Using a dry-brush technique (see bottom of page 97), add white acrylic paint to the page.

3. Tear, wrinkle and sponge orange cardstock with ginger dye ink. Glue pieces to page.

4. Apply rub-on words to three pictures. Glue pictures to page with fabric mesh under some of the corners.

5. Insert mini brads into silk flower centers and glue flowers and velvet leaves to page.

6. Place Defined Words behind copper metal frame. Add twine and ribbon; adhere to page.

7. Apply bubble letter to copper metal charm. Add mini brad and twine; glue to page.

8. Add safety pins to paper scraps and adhere scraps to page.

9. Lastly, apply "Happiness" rub-on to bottom of page.

I just love your eyes sweet Charlie! You are so full of life and wonder and it is a pleasure to spend time with you. I remember when you just smiled a lot and did not speak much.
Funny, you just waited until you had something important to say and now you chatter a bunch.
You're a beautiful girl, Charlie and I look forward to getting to
know you as you grow into a young lady! I love you!

CHaRLie

CHARLIE

Roben-Marie Smith

MATERIALS

RUBBER STAMPS: Foam Stamps by Making Memories

PAPERS: Pink Strawberry Cream by Basic-Grey; Black and White by 7gypsies

PAINTS: White Acrylic Paint by Delta

WORDS, LETTERS OR STICKERS: Chipboard Letters "C" and "L" by Heidi Swapp; Remaining Letters by Li'l Davis Designs

TRANSPARENCIES: Local Office Supply

METAL ITEMS: Black Photo Turns by 7gypsies; Black Mini Brads by American Tag

ADHESIVES: Glue Stick; Glue Dots by Glue Dots International; Diamond Glaze by Judi-Kins

OTHER: Text Paper from Book; Stitched Border by Li'l Davis Designs; Pink Silk Flowers by Making Memories

TOOLS: Paint Brush; Hole Punch by Fiskars

INSTRUCTIONS

1. Using a dry-brush technique, brush white acrylic paint over pink strawberry scrapbook paper.

2. Computer-generate words and print onto transparency. Adhere to top of page with Diamond Glaze.

3. Tear black word paper and adhere to middle of page.

4 Glue old text paper from book to center of black word paper.

5. Adhere photo to page and attach black photo turns with mini brads.

6. Paint "C" chipboard letter with white acrylic paint and adhere to page with Glue Dots.

7. Using decorative foam stamps and white acrylic paint, stamp image around picture.

8. Adhere remaining letters with Glue Dots; add silk flower behind the letter "a" for a decorative touch.

9. Peel off backing and adhere "stitched" strip to bottom of page.

Charlie is my niece and she inspires me! She is such a cute little girl I can't help but want to use photos of her in my work. I took this picture of her while she was watching television. She was so focused on the program that it was easy to capture her without her moving around.

ME & MOM

Roben-Marie Smith

My mom is very young looking and often when we are out together people think we are sisters. I love this photograph because my mom looks so pretty and happy! She was visiting me in Florida and we wanted to have a picture taken of the two of us together. This was our favorite shot… taken by me, holding the camera out in front of us!

MATERIALS

PAPERS: Striped and Script Paper by K&Company; Botanical Paper by Rusty Pickle; Cardstock: Local Craft Store

WORDS, LETTERS OR STICKERS: Defined Word Stickers by Making Memories; Bingo Words by Li'l Davis Designs

METAL ITEMS: Eyelets and Copper Mini Brads: Local Craft Store

ADHESIVES: Glue Stick; Glue Dots by Glue Dots International

TOOLS: Eyelet Setter; Small Paint Brush; 1/8" Hole Punch by Fiskars

OTHER: Old Text Papers; Twine; Lace; Silk Flowers; Velvet Leaves by ARTchix Studio

INSTRUCTIONS

1. Using very little paint and a dry brush, use a dry-brush technique (see bottom of page 97) to paint dark brown piece of cardstock with white acrylic paint.

2. Cut and layer striped, script, botanical paper and old text papers and glue to page.

3. Layer photo to script paper and glue to page.

4. Add mini brads to silk flowers for centers; adhere flowers and leaves to page with Glue Dots.

5. Punch holes in various places and add eyelets.

6. Tie twine through some eyelets and tie in a knot. Stretch some of the twine across the page to tie off.

7. Adhere bingo words to page with Glue Dots.

8. Apply "Cherish" sticker to page.

BRIANNA
Roben-Marie Smith

MATERIALS

PAPERS: Floral Paper by Anna Griffin; Plaid Paper by K&Company; School Book Paper by Li'l Davis Designs

WORDS, LETTERS OR STICKERS: Sticker Words by Pebbles, Inc.; Sticker Word in White by Bo-Bunny Press; Number Stickers by Li'l Davis Designs

TAGS: Printed Tags by FoofaLa; Black Coin Tag by Making Memories

METAL ITEMS: Label Holder and Jump Ring by Making Memories; Photo Turns by 7gypsies; Safety Pin by Li'l Davis Designs; Black Mini Brads: Local Craft Store

RIBBONS: Local Craft Store

ADHESIVES: Glue Stick; Glue Dots by Glue Dots International

OTHER: Vintage Buttons; Twine; Beads; Silk Flowers

TOOLS: Stapler; Dymo Labelmaker

INSTRUCTIONS

1. Cut and glue floral and plaid paper to page.

2. Mount photo to plaid paper; trim and add to page.

3. Add ribbon to page.

4. Cut printed tags; add mini brads and photo turns to the hole in two of them. Glue printed tags to bottom right of page.

5. Apply sticker words to page.

6. Thread beads onto twine; tie through holes in metal label holder and secure to page.

7. Adhere white sticker to black tag and secure to twine with safety pin and jump ring.

8. Add scraps of floral paper to page with staples.

9. Adhere silk flowers to page with Glue Dots and add a vintage button to the center of each flower.

10. Using a Dymo Labelmaker, emboss a custom label and add to page.

I have watched Brianna grow into a sweet young lady over the past seven years. She certainly has her own style and had on the cutest outfit the day I took this photo. I thought the hat was a nice touch, and so vogue! She enjoyed having her picture taken and her easy-going personality made for a fun photo session.

CHERISH

Roben-Marie Smith

MATERIALS

PAPERS: Ochre by Paper Adventures; Green "The Road We Take" by Jeneva & Company; Prospect by 7gypsies; Corrugated by Graphic Products Corporation

PAINTS: Black Acrylic by Liquitex

RUB-ONS: EZ Transfer Words by Jeneva & Company

ADHESIVES: Glue Stick

OTHER: Black Stencil Letter by Autumn Leaves; Green Crayon by Crayola; Text Paper from Old Book; Record Divider

INSTRUCTIONS

1. Using black acrylic paint, imprint a record divider with the pattern on the corrugated paper, using it like a stamp.

2. Adhere the record divider to the ochre paper and attach to front of green scrapbook paper.

3. Attach Prospect paper to center of divider and add picture.

4. Back a "C" stencil with old text paper and adhere to bottom of picture.

5. Cut a scrap of text paper and glue to right-hand side of page; glue a small piece to the side of the picture.

6. Adhere rub-on words to lower right corner of ochre paper.

This is a photograph of my friend Renee's two children. It was taken on the beach in Miami. This precious image makes you feel the warmth and caring an older sister can have for her younger brother. The photo is more meaningful and has more impact because of what we don¹t see.

Carolyn spent the early years of her life coloring in coloring books, and cutting, pasting and creating with construction paper, never realizing that her childhood play would evolve into a lifelong passion. "I love this hobby and feel so blessed to be involved with this publication," she says emphatically. Her layouts have also been published in *Paper Crafts, Memory Makers, Legacy, Canadian Scrapbooker, Woman's Day Scrapbooking* and *Paper Trends* as well as in idea books for Chatterbox and Rusty Pickle. She has designed paper lines for Rusty Pickle and is currently the Senior Creative Director at Melissa Frances.

On any given day, you can find Carolyn in her comfy sweats, hair all awry, scrapbooking her heart out with her two Bichon Frise dogs looking on. She has been known to scour flea markets and stalk auctions on eBay in her quest to add to her collections of old books, vintage photos and beautiful fabrics. Carolyn loves to spend her free time with her police officer husband who has supported her crafting for eight years.

JASON *Carolyn Peeler*

MATERIALS

PAPERS: Taupe Brocade Background by Anna Griffin; Blue and Cream Floral Dot by Melissa Frances; Blue Baby Boy Paper by me and my BIG ideas; Blue Cardstock by Bazzill Basics

PAINTS: White and Blue Acrylic Paints by Delta

WORDS, LETTERS OR STICKERS: Letters "A" and "N" by Doodlebug Design; "S" and "J": Local Craft Store

METAL ITEMS: Flower and Molding by Making Memories; Letter "O": Local Craft Store

RIBBONS: May Arts

FABRICS: Remnant: Local Home Décor or Fabric Store; White Netting: Local Craft or Fabric Store

OTHER: Paper Flower by Making Memories; Vintage Button

INSTRUCTIONS

1. Cut blue baby boy patterned paper to 3 ¾" x 11". Glue to bottom of blue cardstock.

2. Cut taupe brocade to 4 ½" x 10 ½" inches. Glue directly above baby boy paper, centering it on the page.

3. Cut blue floral dot paper to 6" x 3". Glue to right side of layout.

4. Use white paint to whitewash the papers, the edge of your photo, the metal molding and your metal letter. Paint the metal flower blue.

5. Glue fabric to right side of paper.

6. Adhere photo on top of fabric.

7. Layer flowers onto bottom right of photo in the following order: metal flower, netting flower, paper flower and button threaded with sheer ribbon.

8. Apply letters to spell out child's name on the bottom left of the layout.

9. Glue molding across the bottom of the layout.

I was so excited when I found out that my brother and his wife were expecting their second child; I couldn't wait to hold the baby and cuddle it close. When little Jason arrived, I was honored to be asked to take his photo for the birth announcements. This is my favorite photo from that photo shoot. I love how soft and new he looks wrapped in the blanket his Grandma made. I hope this layout conveys how truly treasured Jason is.

U at 2

2004

july

I Love You

U AT 2
Carolyn Peeler

MATERIALS

RUBBER STAMPS: Bold Alphabet by JoAnn Essentials; Printers Type Alphabet by Hero Arts

DYE INKPADS: Light Brown: Local Craft Store

PAPERS: "Annabelle" Red Striped Paper and "Emily" Floral Paper by Melissa Frances; Cream Cardstock: Local Craft Store

PAINTS: Antique White and Deep Red: Local Craft Store

WORDS, LETTERS OR STICKERS: Red Flower by Nostalgiques by EK Success; Red Label Sticker: Local Craft Store

RUB-ONS: Month Rub-On by Li'l Davis Designs

TAGS: Local Craft Store

MESH: Local Craft or Fabric Store

RIBBONS: Local Craft Store

ADHESIVES: Liquid Glue; Mono Adhesive by Tombow

OTHER: Lace; Shell Button; Red Thread; Red Flower; Metal Corner; Vellum Envelope by Anna Griffin; Cream Tab by Melissa Frances

TOOLS: Needle; Paint Brush; Sewing Machine

INSTRUCTIONS

1. Cut Emily paper to 3 ½" x 11". Ink edges with light brown ink. Glue to the bottom of the red 8 ½" x 11" paper.

2. Cut Annabelle paper to ¾" x 11". Ink edges with light brown ink. Glue to the bottom of the Emily paper.

3. Dip your finger in antique white acrylic paint and run it along the four edges of the 8 ½" x 11" sheet, reapplying paint to your finger as needed. Tie cream and red ribbon to the interface between the Annabelle and Emily papers.

4. Dip your paint brush in red acrylic paint and run it along the four edges of the vellum envelope, reapplying paint as needed. Attach the corner accent to the top left side of the vellum envelope.

5. Use a combination of rubber stamps and handwriting for "U at 2" title on the red label sticker. Glue label onto vellum envelope.

6. Use red thread to machine-stitch a flower shape onto some old lace. Once you have created the flower, cut the shape out of the lace. Cut a flower shape out of mesh; glue on top of the lace flower.

7. Glue red flower to the top of the mesh; sew a shell button to the center of the red flower. Glue assembled lace flower and adhere flower sticker onto the vellum envelope.

8. Stamp date on the cream Melissa Frances tab.

9. Slightly distress the edges of your photo with white acrylic paint. Glue cream Melissa Frances tab behind the upper right side of the photo.

10. Apply date rub-on to the bottom right of the photo. Glue photo onto layout.

I love how serious and studied this little face is in this layout. Even the happiest child can have moments of serious contemplation. I felt honored to be given this photo to scrap from my friend Dee who is an extraordinary photographer

They say that a happy child is a joy to behold, and as soon as I saw this photo that my friend Dee took of her daughter, a big smile came to my face. I wanted to create a layout that captured her happiness and expressed how joyful it made me feel to see her smile. Her cute little smile lights up the entire page!

YOU MAKE ME SMILE

Carolyn Peeler

MATERIALS

RUBBER STAMPS: Antique Type by PSX; Bold Alphabet by JoAnn Essentials; Printers Type Alphabet by Hero Arts

DYE INKPADS: Light Brown: Local Craft Store

PAPERS: Pink Circle Dot Paper by FoofaLa; "Cole" Green Striped Paper by Melissa Frances; Pink and Cream Cardstock: Local Craft Store

PAINTS: Antique White, Taupe, Pink and Burnt Umber

WORDS, LETTERS OR STICKERS: 100% Girl by DieCuts with a View

TAGS: "Anne" Green Polka Dot Tag by Melissa Frances; Pink Tag: Local Craft Store

METAL ITEMS: Paper Clip by Nostalgiques by EK Success; Bookplate and Pink Eyelet: Local Craft Store

RIBBONS: Ribbons and Trim: Local Craft Store

ADHESIVES: Mono Adhesive by Tombow

OTHER: Green Fence Card by Memory Box; Chipboard Letters and Flower Tape by Heidi Swapp; Green Tab by Melissa Frances

TOOLS: Sewing Machine; Paper Trimmer; Eyelet Setter; Metal Alphabet Stamps; Hammer; Paint Brush; Pencil; Blending Gel Medium

INSTRUCTIONS

1. Cut Cole paper to 5" x 12". Cut pink cardstock to 4 ½" x 9". Use white acrylic paint to dry brush (see bottom of page 97) the pink cardstock, giving it a white-washed appearance.

2. Antique the edges of the pink dot background paper, the Cole patterned paper and the pink cardstock with light brown ink.

3. Glue the striped paper, pink cardstock and pink dot patterned paper as shown. Distress edge of photo with white acrylic paint. Glue green Melissa Frances tab behind the lower right side of the photo. Attach chipboard letter to the top left of the photo. Glue photo to layout.

4. Adhere a strip of the Heidi Swapp tape to the bottom of the layout; glue white dress trim under the floral tape and pink ribbon on top. Sew the edges where the white trim and floral tape meet, alternating between a straight and zigzag stitch.

5. Paint white dots on the Memory Box card. When the paint is dry, draw a circle around the dots with a pencil.

Machine-stitch the card shut to create a pocket. Antique the edges with light brown ink. Attach paper clip to the left side of your card/pocket and glue to page

6. Create two tags to go inside the pocket. One tag should contain your journaling; the other tag, a DieCuts With a View sticker. Distress edges of the tags using acrylic paint and light brown ink. Attach ribbons to tags; insert tags in pocket.

7. Stamp date in metal bookplate using metal stamps. Paint metal bookplate with antique white acrylic paint; let dry and apply gel medium. Once dry, rub in burnt umber paint to highlight each letter/number. When completely dry, glue plate to layout, as shown.

8. Stamp the word "happy" onto the Melissa Frances tab, as shown.

9. Computer-generate title and print out; cut title to size. Distress edges with pink acrylic paint and glue to layout, as shown.

Cherish

CHILD

fond memorie's

baby (bā bē), *n.* an infant or very
young child; the youngest or the
smallest member of a family or
group; a term of endearment.

cute BABY

PRECIOUS *life*

PRECIOUS (presh′-es) 1. of great worth. 2. beloved-cherished

CAROLYN

RUTH

ANDERSON

open book

CAROLYN RUTH ANDERSON
Carolyn Peeler

MATERIALS

RUBBER STAMPS: Hydrangea and Old Label by Anna Griffin for All Night Media/Plaid; Baby Definition by Catslife Press; Small Letter in Script by Penny Black Rubber Stamps; Antique Alphabet by PSX

PIGMENT INKPADS: Pink, Red and Green: Local Craft Store

DYE INKPADS: Light Brown and Dark Brown: Local Craft Store

PAPERS: Old Buttons Paper by K&Company; Pink Stripes by Anna Griffin; Baby Words Paper in White and Pink: Computer-Generated; White Cardstock: Local Craft Store

PAINTS: White and Pink: Local Craft Store

WORDS, LETTERS OR STICKERS: Flowers and Key by Nostalgiques by EK Success; Defined Words by Making Memories

RUB-ONS: Making Memories

TAGS: Local Office Supply

METAL ITEMS: White Square Bookplate by Making Memories

ADHESIVES: Mono Adhesive by Tombow

OTHER: Brown Embroidery Floss; Natural Twill from Old Piece of Linen or Burlap; Vintage Buttons

TOOLS: Paper Cutter; Needle; Bristle Paint Brush; Sandpaper

INSTRUCTIONS

1. Cut two sheets of pink striped paper to 8" x 8" each.

2. Cut two pieces of button paper: one 6 ½" x 4" and the other 1 ½" x 5".

3. Cut two pieces of pink baby paper: one 3" x 8" and the other 3" x 6 ½".

4. Ink edges of all cut papers.

5. Stamp baby definition onto white cardstock using light brown ink; ink edges.

6. Stamp hydrangea onto white cardstock using pink and green ink; ink edges.

7. Stamp old label in pink ink onto white cardstock. Trim around the stamped image. Use dark brown ink to stamp text onto the label.

8. Stamp "open book" with alphabet stamps onto a scrap of white cardstock.

9. Stamp "cute baby" onto tag with light brown ink; ink edges.

10. Use white acrylic paint to slightly distress the edges of photo; apply rub-ons as shown. Attach a Defined Word sticker that includes the word "child" to the top left corner of the photo (much like a photo corner) so that the word "child" shows.

11. Type the name of the person in the photo in a computer program (using a taupe background and white text) then print out. Trim the names down and ink the edges.

12. To create the booklet for the right side of the layout, cut a piece of white cardstock to 4 ½" x 7" and fold in half. Glue white Baby Words paper to the cover and trim edges. Sew Old Buttons paper to bottom of the booklet. Add Nostalgiques floral, key sticker and definition sticker as shown. Add a small white bookplate with the stamped words "open book" glued behind it. Sew vintage buttons onto top left.

This layout is close and dear to my heart. This is my husband's mother as a small baby. It's often difficult to think of one's parents as infants, yet that's how each of us started. I used the combination of pink, which is soft, new and bright, with old vintage buttons to give a sense of vintage chic to this layout.

mothers

daughters

grandmothers

I think it's important to honor women and the way they pass stories, memories and traditions down through the family. I can trace my foremothers back to the Magna Carta, but the photos only go back so far. I used one of my rescued cabinet photos to represent all of my unphotographed ancestors and then surrounded it with photos of my grandmother, mother, sister and daughters. I'm the middle one on the left, circa 1970.

*B*est known for her Fragment Series of small fabric collages, Lesley is also a nationally known quilter and mixed-media artist with a passion for color and the written word. Her work takes the form of art quilts, fabric books, dolls and more. She has taught from coast-to-coast and her art and articles have appeared in numerous publications and juried shows. Her art and writing focus on her passion – the inspiration and creativity of women. In her current position as Arts Editor of the new magazine *Cloth Paper Scissors*, Lesley hopes to showcase new talent and mixed media art. Her first book, *Quilted Memories* (Sterling/Chapelle), brings new ideas and techniques to quilting and preserving memories. She is currently awaiting publication of her second book, *Fabric Memory Books*. With her art and books, Lesley aspires to inspire others to find their own voice and create their art.

MOTHERS/DAUGHTERS/GRANDMOTHERS

Lesley Riley

MATERIALS

PAPERS: Yellow Vine Flocked Paper by K&Company

FABRICS: Inkjet-Printable Fabric by ColorTextiles; Vintage Fabrics and Lace: Local Fabric Store

ADHESIVES: PeelnStick by Therm O Web

OTHER: Sticky Stitches by Colorbok

TOOLS: Sewing Machine

INSTRUCTIONS

1. Follow ColorTextiles package instructions to print photos and words onto fabric; cut out.

2. Follow package instructions to apply PeelnStick to fabric.

3. Machine-sew and assemble work as shown.

DUCK POND *Lesley Riley*

MATERIALS

FABRICS: Inkjet-Printable Fabric by Color-Textiles; Indian Silks: Local Fabric Store

RIBBONS: Ruban by 7gypsies

ADHESIVES: PeelnStick by Therm O Web

OTHER: Vintage Buttons

TOOLS: Sewing Machine

INSTRUCTIONS

1. Follow ColorTextiles package instructions to print photos and words onto fabric; cut out.

2. Follow package instructions to apply PeelnStick to fabric.

3. Machine-sew and assemble work as shown.

My son sure knows how to take a great photo. Everything about this one was perfect, and so were the Indian sari fabrics I brought back from my trip to Vancouver, BC. To pick up the pink in the girl's dress, I threaded silk ribbon from 7gypsies through three mother of pearl buttons — one for each child.

A Close Inspection

When was the last time you spent a quiet moment just doing nothing – just sitting and looking at the sea, or watching the wind blowing the tree limbs, or waves rippling on a pond, a flickering candle or children playing in the park? Ralph Marston

Boston Common

Town Hall

Duck Pond

A dream is a wish your heart makes, when you're fast asleep.

FAST ASLEEP

Lesley Riley

MATERIALS

FABRICS: Inkjet-Printable Fabric by ColorTextiles; Vintage Fabric and Lace: Local Fabric Store

ADHESIVES: PeelnStick by Therm O Web

TOOLS: Sewing Machine

INSTRUCTIONS

1. Follow ColorTextiles package instructions to print photos and words onto fabric; cut out.

2. Follow package instructions to apply PeelnStick to fabric.

3. Machine-sew and assemble work as shown.

TIP Make this into an adorable pillow for a precious gift idea.

I'm biased of course, but I think my granddaughters look like angels even when they are awake. But asleep – well there's no doubt about it. I was having trouble finding something that would work with this photo. It called for something dramatic, yet feminine and delicate. When I reached into my stash of vintage laces, I knew I had found just the right combination to make this photo sing.

CAMERA CLUB

Lesley Riley

MATERIALS

FABRICS: Inkjet-Printable Fabric by ColorTextiles; Camera Fabric by Rainbow Resource; Black Felt and Cotton Fabric: Local Fabric Store

ADHESIVES: PeelnStick by Therm O Web

OTHER: Photograph Negatives

TOOLS: Sewing Machine

INSTRUCTIONS

1. Follow ColorTextiles package instructions to print photos and words onto fabric; cut out.

2. Follow package instructions to apply PeelnStick to fabric.

3. Machine-sew and assemble work as shown.

I once had a friend who collected old cameras. It was wonderful to see them so artistically arranged all together. When I found this photo of a women's camera club, I knew just how I wanted to handle it. I had purchased the camera fabric on a whim, knowing that it would one day come in handy. The whole page just came together so perfectly.

TIP *Add a frame for a finishing touch!*

*A*my maintains a full-time technical career by day, but has also been teaching classes in paper arts since 2001. In addition to several TweetyJill publications, her work has been featured in *Somerset Studios, Return to Asia, Rubber Stamper, Expressions,* and *Stamper's Sampler.* Amy teaches primarily in Phoenix, Arizona but has also taught in New England and California.

Her art is ever evolving; she's always trying something new. Her most enjoyable venture of late is giving new life to familiar techniques with bold splashes of color. Raised in an artistic household, she was always encouraged to create. "There was no escaping art," she says, "and I wouldn't want to anyway." Amy lives in Peoria, Arizona with her husband George and their "cat-child" Twitch.

STUDIO TIME

Amy Wellenstein

MATERIALS

PAPERS: Pink Cardstock by Making Memories; Megan's Room (Polka Dots) by Deluxe Designs; Black Paper by Fibermark

WORDS, LETTERS OR STICKERS: So Bold Cardstock Stickers (Pink) by SEI; Simply Chic (Milan Black) Alphabet Stickers by American Crafts; Vinyl Alphabet Stickers (Black on White): Local Hardware Store

ADHESIVES: Scotch Double-Stick Tape by 3M

TOOLS: Sandpaper

INSTRUCTIONS

1. Assemble photographs in the lower right corner to create a mosaic of your focal image.

2. Adhere pink cardstock stickers to spell out the word "STUDIO" along the lower left side.

3. Sand the edges of a piece of polka dot paper. Adhere black alphabet stickers to spell out the word "TIME" and tape to page.

4. Use vinyl stickers to spell out "IS TIME TO CREATE" on pink cardstock. Cut the words apart and adhere across the top of the page.

I created this layout as a reminder that I have TOO MUCH STUFF! I keep telling myself "you just need more storage"... but I have no room for storage! I truly believe that I spend more time organizing my supplies than I do using them. When my friends come over to make art, they're always so impressed at how everything is labeled. If they only knew that the labels haven't matched what's in the drawers for months!

VINTAGE RIDE

Amy Wellenstein

MATERIALS

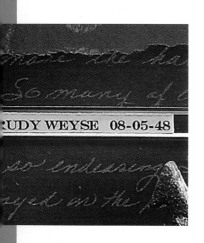

PAPERS: Arithmetique by 7gyp-sies; Designer Silver Script by DieCuts with a View; Black Card-stock: Local Craft Store

WORDS, LETTERS OR STICK-ERS: CRE8-A-PLATE License Plate and Road Trip Alphabet Stickers by Sticker Studio

METAL ITEMS: Black Aluminum Screen: Local Hardware Store; Sil-ver Eyelets: Local Craft Store; Prong Fastener: Local Office Supply

ADHESIVES: Glue Stick; Scotch Double-Stick Tape by 3M

TOOLS: Eyelet Setter; Hammer

INSTRUCTIONS

1. Tear a strip of black script paper. Use glue stick to adhere the strip to the bottom of the red page.

2. Create the title with CRE8-A-PLATE stickers.

3. Adhere the title to a piece of black aluminum screen. Use double-stick tape to mount the title on the page.

4. Mount a photo in the center of the page with glue stick and black photo corners..

5. Layer the page onto a sheet of black cardstock.

6. Set silver eyelets around the edge of the page. After setting the eyelets, pound them flat with a hammer to give them the appearance of rivets.

7. Use heavy scissors to trim the prongs off of a prong paper fastener. Insert computer-generated text and glue below the photo as an index plate.

The handsome young gentleman in this layout is my grandfather Rudy. I loved the contrast of the photo and the white writing along the bottom (Cromwell, Conn. Home again. Aug 5, 1948). The CRE8-A-PLATE stickers allowed me to design a custom title. The black metal screen and silver eyelets gave it the masculine touch it needed.

VINTAGE PHOTOS

Amy Wellenstein

MATERIALS

PAPERS: Dream by Daisy D's; Dictionary Thoughts and Dictionary Family by Real Life by Pebbles, Inc.; Musique Kraft-Colored Tissue Paper and Black Index Tab by 7gypsies: Black Cardstock: Local Craft Store

METAL ITEMS: Metal Frame by Metal Memorabilia by Li'l Davis Designs;

Copper Safety Pins: Local Craft Store

ADHESIVES: Scotch Double-Stick Foam Tape by 3M; Embossable Tape Sheets by Amy's Magic

OTHER: Mica by USArtQuest; Twill Alphabet by Paper Bliss by Westrim Crafts

TOOLS: Sewing Machine

TECHNIQUE: Mica Transfer

INSTRUCTIONS

1. Layer several patterned papers for the background, tearing the edges of some for a random collage effect.

2. Cut the ribbon portion from a second sheet of Dream scrapbook paper. Reinforce the ribbon with a strip of black cardstock.

3. Punch small holes along the strip and use safety pins to attach twill letters.

4. Attach the strip to the page using double-stick foam tape.

5. Transfer a vintage photo to a piece of mica using the Mica Transfer Technique

6. Use a sewing machine to stitch the mica transfer to the page.

7. Layer printed tissue on a rectangle of black cardstock; use brads to attach a small photo and metal frame. Embellish with an index tab, then adhere to page.

The couple in striped shirts are my maternal grandparents, Rudy and Nancy. My great grandfather Otto is seated next to them on the stone wall. For as far back as I can remember, my Grandpa Rudy has always collected rock specimens, crystals and minerals. I recall one time in my childhood that he gave me a flat of stones labeled with their proper names... I thought it was TREASURE! It seemed only fitting to use mica in this layout, as Grandpa Rudy gave me my first piece.

NORTH FORK

Amy Wellenstein

MATERIALS

PAPERS: Alphabet Background by Paper Loft; Nature Patterned Paper by Autumn Leaves; Green Cardstock by Bazzill Basics; Elm-Olive Vellum by Liz King by EK Success

WORDS, LETTERS OR STICKERS: Life's Journey Words (Journey) by K&Company; Dictionary Travel Strips and Travel Labels (Rest), Nature Sampler (Leaves), Family Bits & Pieces (Tag), and Love Bits & Pieces (Envelope) by Real Life by Pebbles Inc.; Defined Words (Journey)

by Making Memories; Window Keeper by Nostalgiques from The Attic Collection by EK Success

METAL ITEMS: Brown Photo Turns by 7gypsies; Brads: Local Craft Store

ADHESIVES: Glue Stick; Scotch Double-Stick Tape by 3M; Embossable Tape Sheets by Amy's Magic

OTHER: Clear Embossing Powder; Letterpress Twill by 7gypsies

TOOLS: Sewing Machine; Sandpaper

INSTRUCTIONS

1. Layer vellum over background paper. Mount on cardstock for stability.

2. Adhere sticker borders across the top and bottom of the page. Embellish the top border with leaf stickers.

3. Cut out letters from patterned paper. Use embossable tape sheets and clear embossing powder to emboss the surface of the letters. Use the letters to spell out the title of the page.

4. Sand the edges of two photographs and secure them to the page using double-stick tape. Stitch around the photos.

5. Use brads to attach photo turns to one of the photos. Stitch the "Destination" definition to the bottom of the same photo.

6. Trim a third photo to fit in a window keeper. Layer the window keeper on the page with several coordinating stickers as shown.

7. Stitch along the edges of the page.

8. Staple on a piece of printed twill tape to finish the layout.

My husband and I took a day trip to North Fork (north of where we live in Arizona). It was such a relaxing day, and so nice just to rest under this shady tree. This is a pleasant reminder of that cool, calm day.

Sarah started taking English riding lessons when she was six years old. At 16, she still loves them and has even been privileged to own several horses. Now she has progressed to jumpers and shows competitively in the jumper classes. Here she is on her beautiful horse.

Jill Haglund is a prolific author and artist who loves scrapbooking, paper crafts, rubber stamping and all things mixed media. As founder and president of TweetyJill Publications, she has produced and self-published ten books and is currently working on her latest, *Rubber Stamped Artists Trading Cards (ATCs)*. These days you can find her up in her studio until the wee hours, having a grand time dabbling and creating ATCs for this fun new title.

Jill is often chosen to speak at industry conventions, where she entertains eager audiences with her easy smile and clever sense of humor. She has also conducted national workshops and demonstrated and instructed at conventions, trade shows and retail stores.

Teaching is one of the most fulfilling aspects of her craft; unleashing the creativity of others and helping them discover the freedom to express themselves gives her great joy.

With a warm and whimsical flair, she gently "pushes the envelope," causing her students' self-expectations — and imaginations — to soar… a guaranteed formula for success that is reflected in each of her publications.

Her greatest passion is showcasing other artists' work in her books for readers to enjoy, replicate and gather ideas to create their own unique pieces.

Jill and her very supportive family live in Sarasota, Florida with "Rusty," their loveable Golden Retriever.

SARAH JOY *Jill Haglund*

MATERIALS

PIGMENT INKPADS: Brown: Local Craft Store

DYE INKPADS: Brown: Local Craft Store

PAPERS: Lollipop, Aged and Confused Sublime Collection; Vintage Rose and Cinnamon by BasicGrey; Word Definitions Paper by Jenny Bowlin

WORDS, LETTERS OR STICKERS: Joy Definition by Wild Asparagus by My Mind's Eye

METAL ITEMS: Turquoise Brads: Local Craft Store

RIBBONS: Hand-Dyed Silk Ribbon by 7gypsies

ADHESIVES: Scotch Double-Stick Tape by 3M; The Ultimate! Glue by Crafter's Pick

TOOLS: 1/8" Hole Punch, Quickuts Tool by Provo Craft; Ruler; Pencil

INSTRUCTIONS

1. Tear papers; rub edges with pigment ink to distress and layer as shown for background.

2. Ink around the edge of photo with dye ink and adhere to layout.

3. Use a ruler and pencil to mark left-hand side at one-inch internals all the way down. Punch holes at each mark and insert brads.

4. To make tags: Cut out definitions from Jenny Bowlin paper, tape to striped paper and trim. Punch holes in top; set an eyelet and thread ribbon through each. Glue to page.

5. Ink Joy definition and tape to page.

6. Use Quickuts tool to press out font to spell "Sarah"; glue to page on top of Joy definition to represent name "Sarah Joy".

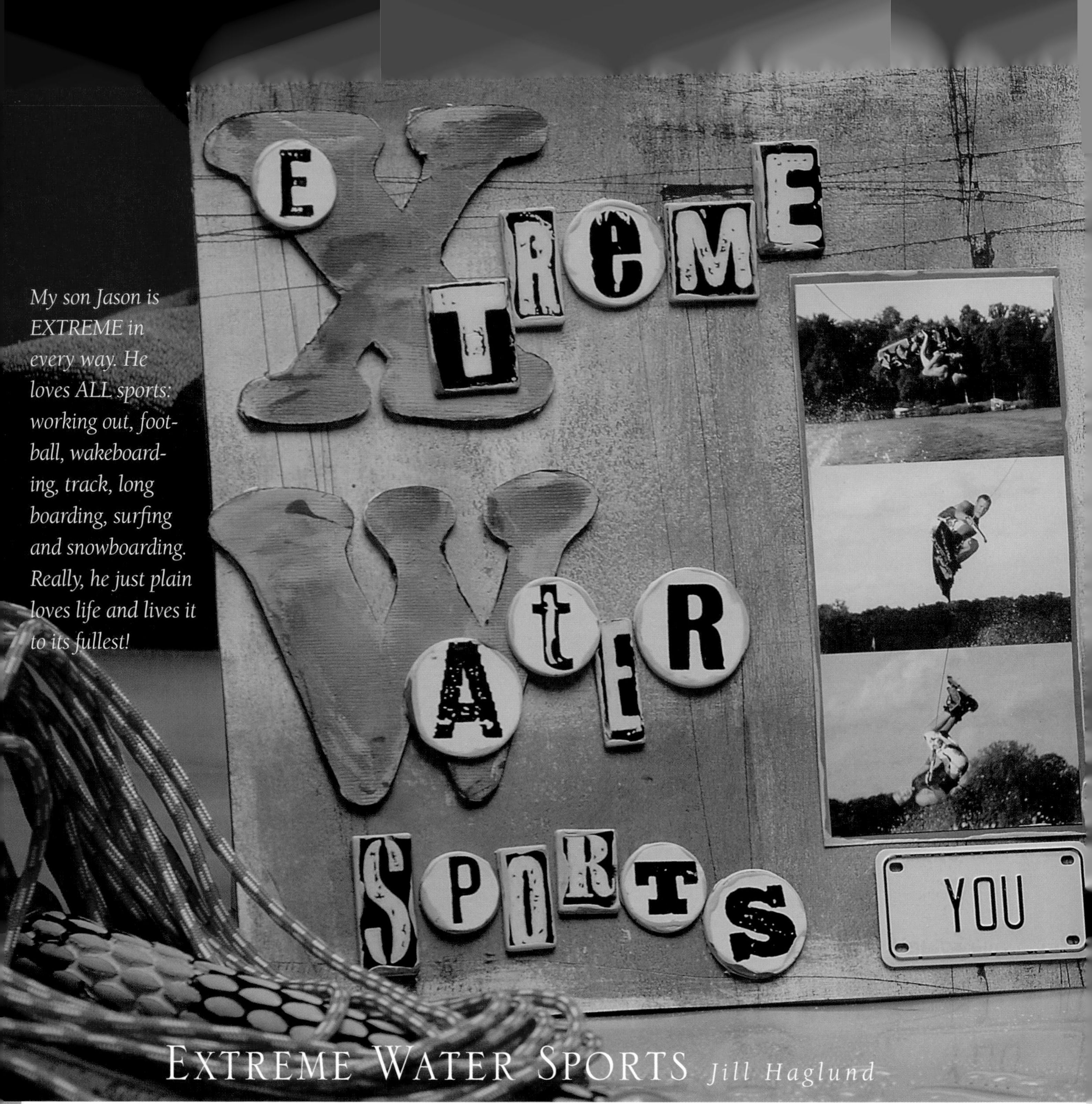

My son Jason is EXTREME in every way. He loves ALL sports: working out, football, wakeboarding, track, long boarding, surfing and snowboarding. Really, he just plain loves life and lives it to its fullest!

EXTREME WATER SPORTS *Jill Haglund*

MATERIALS

DYE INKPADS: Brown: Local Craft Store

PAPERS: "Live with intention, play with abandon" and Cinnamon Paper by BasicGrey; Blue and Terra Cotta Cardstock: Local Craft Store

PAINTS: Blue and White Acrylic: Local Craft Store

WORDS, LETTERS OR STICKERS: Alphabet Chipboard Letters in Circles and Squares by Li'l Davis

Designs; Extra Large "X" and "W": Local Craft Store

METAL ITEMS: Alphadotz and Hugz by Scrapworks; "TIME", "YOU" and "2006": Local Craft Store

TAGS: Local Craft Store

ADHESIVES: Scotch Double-Stick Tape by 3M; The Ultimate! Glue by Crafter's Pick

TOOLS: Small Paint Brush

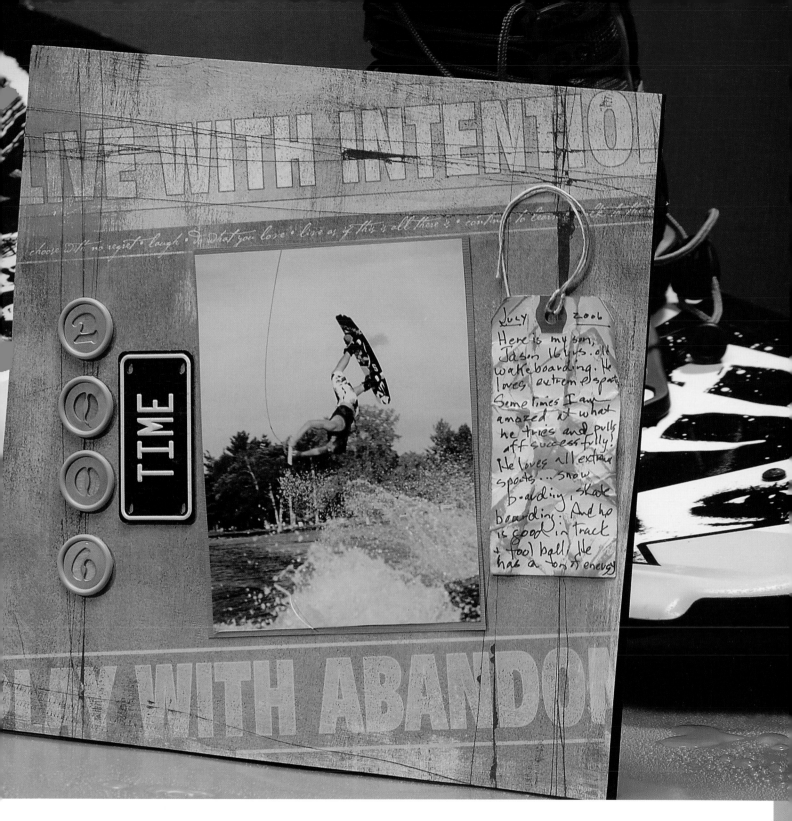

INSTRUCTIONS

1. Use two BasicGrey papers as background.

2. Paint large letters "E" and "W" with blue paint; add white paint here and there. Sand edges of letters. Attach to page for title.

3. Use a paint brush to paint a blue edge on smaller chipboard letters. Adhere on top of and following large letters to finish the title, "Extreme Water Sports".

4. Glue "TIME" and "YOU" plates to pages.

5. Place terra cotta cardstock behind numbers for date "2006" and glue to page.

6. Mat photo collage with blue cardstock and paint edge of mat. Mat large photo onto blue cardstock. Adhere all photos to page.

7. Lastly, journal onto tag; crumple tag, then rub lightly with brown ink to distress as shown. Attach to page.

ERIC
Jill Hagland

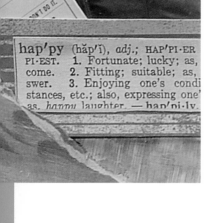

MATERIALS

DYE INKPADS: Light Blue: Local Craft Store

PAPER: Lollipop Shoppe by BasicGrey

PAINT: Gold Acrylic: Local Craft Store

MARKERS: Size .05 Marking Pen: Local Craft Store

WORDS, LETTERS OR STICKERS: Cardstock Perforated Letters by Basic Grey; Stickers by Creative Imaginations; Definition by Jenny Bowlin

TAG: Evidence Tag by 7gypsies

ADHESIVES: Scotch Double-Sided Tape by 3M; The Ultimate! Glue by Crafter's Pick; Glue Dots by Glue Dots International

OTHER: Wooden "2"

INSTRUCTIONS

1. Use teal blue paper as background. Tear light blue paper into "waves" and tape to page, leaving a small pocket on the top of waves as shown.

2. Sand 5" x 7" photo and tuck into pocket, adhering with tape.

3. Journal onto "Evidence" tag; add blue thumbprints using dye ink. Tuck into pocket.

4. Cut out chosen definition and place onto Lollipop Shoppe paper. Tuck into pocket in front of tag as shown.

5. Use Glue Dots to place the name on layout.

6. Add all stickers to page.

7. Paint the "2" gold and glue to page with The Ultimate! Glue. Dry overnight.

This is my nephew, Eric, solo "barefooting." My sons are the same age as my nephews and they do a lot of things together. They all enjoy the time in the summer wakeboarding at our home on the lake in Minnesota. Eric hasn't seen the picture yet, so I am excited to give this to him as a Christmas gift this year. I thought it would be nice to capture a favorite pastime in his young adult life.

TIP

When you frame them, scrapbook layouts make great gifts for those hard to buy for people on your list, like sons, daughters, nephews and nieces, parents and grandparents!

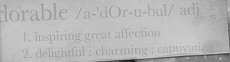

Adorable /a-'dOr-u-bul/ adj.

1. inspiring great affection
2. delightful : charming : captivating

always smilN

You steal my heart each time yo's smile every time I see that sweet grin, it brings a smile to my face. Your personality always cheers me 'p...you brighten my day. Thank y J for spreading joy and reminding me to live in the present.

MegAn

MEGAN MATILDA

Jill Haglund

MATERIALS

PAPERS: Pink with White Dots by American Traditional Designs; Sunny Leaf by Creative Imaginations; Pink Traditional Library Pocket by Daisy D's; Floral: Local Craft Store

PAINTS: Pink Acrylic: Local Craft Store

WORDS, LETTERS OR STICKERS: Phrase Cafe (Always Smiling) by EK Success; Green "Schizophrenic" Chipboard Letters by Heidi Swapp; Chipboard Letter "A" by Li'l Davis Designs; Adorable Definition by Wild Asparagus by My Mind's Eye

METAL ITEMS: Spiral Easel Photo Holder and Heart Clip by 7gypsies; Lime Green and Pink Brads, Photos Turns and Pink Clip: Local Craft Store

RIBBONS: Ribbons, Rick Rack and Trims: Local Craft Store

ADHESIVES: Scotch Double-Stick Tape by 3M; Glue Dots by Glue Dots International; The Ultimate! Glue by Crafter's Pick; E-6000 by Eclectic Products

OTHER: Small Pink Bulldog Clip; Small Magenta Spiral Clip; Magenta and Lime; Green Safety Pins; Silk Flowers

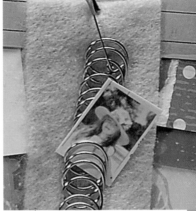

INSTRUCTIONS

1.   Tear papers; tape to page for background.

2.   Place 5" x 7" photo on page. Double-mat the four small photos and position on top right of page with tape and spiral clip.

3.   Run all ribbons and trims along bottom of page.

4.   Use Glue Dots to apply Heidi Swapp green chipboard letters as shown.

5.   Apply rub-on phrase to pink library pocket card. Adhere card to page with tape and photo turns as shown. Place heart clip under bulldog clip.

6.   Add "Adorable" definition. Paint edges of chipboard "A" with pink paint and adhere to "Adorable" definition with Glue Dots as shown.

7.   Make double and triple silk flowers from small and large silk blossoms; insert colored brads. Adhere flowers to page with Glue Dots.

8.   Use Glue Dots to adhere felt to center of page.

9.   Attach spiral easel to felt with two safety pins; insert mini photo.

Megan is the sweet daughter of a close friend. Every single time I saw this photo at her home I wanted to use it someway on a scrapbook page. One day I asked her if I could have it to copy. I love the way the layout turned out because it is the essence of Megan herself. She is a sweet, tender-hearted, girly girl, always happy, inquisitive and bright as a penny!! Seems she always wears a big smile that is backed by kind words. This photo of her is a little unique, because it shows a little wry smile. But right after the photo was taken she burst into giggles, and was back to herself! You can see it in her eyes!

DAVID & LISA

Jill Haglund

MATERIALS

RUBBER STAMPS: Various Alphabet Rubber Stamps By K&Company and Local Craft Store

DYE INKPADS: Black and Pink: Local Craft Store

PAPERS: Pink Hearts Paper by K&Company; Black and Pink Cardstock: Local Craft Store

PAINTS: Pink Acrylic: Local Craft Store

TAGS: Metal-Rimmed Tags: Local Craft Store

TRANSPARENCIES: K&Company

METAL ITEMS: Ribbon Charm Alphabets by Making Memories; Rhinestone Brads and Silver Decorative Brads: Local Craft Store

RIBBONS: Local Craft Store

FABRICS: Pink Felt: Local Fabric Store

ADHESIVES: Scotch Double-Stick Tape by 3M; Glue Dots by Glue Dots International; The Ultimate! Glue by Crafter's Pick; E-6000 by Eclectic Products

OTHER: Key; Wire Heart; Pink Buttons; Silk Flowers by Making Memories

TOOLS: 1/8 " Punch; Paint Brush

INSTRUCTIONS

1. Layer transparency onto pink hearts paper, then onto pink cardstock.

2. Tear black paper and edge with pink paint. Layer pink paper on top of black paper, then tape photo. Add three pink buttons. Adhere to page with Glue Dots.

3. Cut papers to fit tags and stamps as desired.

4. Tear black paper for title. Thread ribbon charm alphabets onto pink ribbon and glue to page with Glue Dots. Add key with E-6000 on right-hand side. Punch hole on left side and add a tag stamped with "OXO".

5. Make three triple-layer silk flowers; add rhinestone brad to center.

6. Tie large bow with ribbon and add a large flower with Glue Dots.

7. Cut and add three small pink felt pieces to page as shown.

8. Tie three different colored snippets of ribbon onto key; attach to felt with E-6000.

9. Adhere stamped tags with Glue Dots.

10. Stamp key image and attach with brads.

11. Use Glue Dots to add flowers to top right corner of layout and to hold wire heart.

FRNDZ

Jill Haglund

MATERIALS

PIGMENT INKPADS: Terra Cotta: Local Craft Store

PAPERS: Wild Asparagus by My Mind's Eye

METAL ITEMS: Brass Frame and Brass Label Holder by Making Memories; "Frndz" and "My Lif" Plates by Creative Imaginations; Decorative Metal Brads and Photo Corners by K&Company; Small Brass Brads: Local Craft Store

RIBBONS: Ruban by 7gypsies; Trim and Green Fiber: Local Fabric Store

ADHESIVES: Scotch Double-Stick Tape by 3M; Glue Dots by Glue Dots International; The Ultimate! Glue by Crafter's Pick

OTHER: Small Paper Labeled with Names; Flowers from "Got Flowers" by Prima by Martin F./Weber Co.

INSTRUCTIONS

1. Tear and layer all papers for background.
2. Position and adhere photo as desired.
3. Add "FRNDZ" and "MY LIF" metal plates with brass brads.
4. Attach brass plate with brads and insert names on small piece of paper.
5. Use brads to run ribbons and trims down and across page.
6. In some areas, tack the ribbons, trim and fiber with glue to keep them secure.
7. Insert brass brads into layered small ocher-colored flowers. Adhere flowers to page with Glue Dots.

This is a photo of my lovely, sweet daughter Lindsay, a sunny joy in my life. I can't imagine life without her near. I am so blessed because even though she is in college and has moved from home, she lives close by. When she walks in, the room lights up! I don't say this JUST because I am her mama, but because she is bright and cheerful and so much fun to be with, laughing and smiling most of the time! I love you Lindsay!

PROM NIGHT - MATT AND MELISSA

Jill Haglund

Here is my oldest son, Matt, on his senior high school prom night with his girlfriend Melissa. She is such a doll! They both looked stunning on this special evening and were excited for it to begin. I was fortunate they stopped by for a brief moment (to make mom happy), so I could photograph them going out the door with stars in their eyes!

MATERIALS

PIGMENT INKPADS: Orchid: Local Craft Store

PAPERS: Mod

WORDS, LETTERS OR STICKERS: Stickers by Creative Imaginations; "Happiness" Embossed Label: Local Craft Store

RUB-ONS: "Prom" (White): Local Craft Store

TAGS: Local Office Supply

METAL ITEMS: Eyelets, Rhinestone Brad, Rhinestone Clip and Pink Round Frame: Local Craft Store

RIBBONS: Organza: Local Craft Store

ADHESIVES: Scotch Double-Stick Tape by 3M; Glue Dots by Glue Dots International; The Ultimate! Glue by Crafter's Pick

OTHER: Silk Flowers by Making Memories; Pink Label Plate by Creative Imaginations

INSTRUCTIONS

1. Tear and ink papers; adhere to scrapbook page for background.

2. Rub orchid ink here and there on papers.

3. Apply stickers and embossed labels as shown.

4. Journal on rectangular tag; crumple tag and distress with orchid colored ink. Attach tag to page with Glue Dots and rhinestone brad.

5. Insert brads into silk flowers and adhere to layout with Glue Dots.

6. Tie ribbon into bow and press to page with Glue Dots.

7. Use brads to attach pink label plate.

PAIGE & HER BROTHERS

Jill Haglund

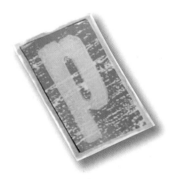

MATERIALS

RUBBER STAMPS: Foam Alphabet by Li'l Davis Designs

PAPERS: Cracked Paint Blue: Local Craft Store

PAINTS: Light Blue and White Acrylic: Local Craft Store

WORDS, LETTERS OR STICKERS: Label Lingo and Phrase Café (Lazy Days, All About Me and Always Smiling) by EK Success

RUB-ONS: Black Words by Making Memories; Colored Rub-Ons

(Expressions Party Mix, All Mixed Up and Swimming Pool) by Doodlebug Design

TAGS: Metal-Rimmed Circle Tags: Local Craft Store

RIBBONS: Local Craft Store

ADHESIVES: Glue Dots by Glue Dots International

OTHER: Pink Ghost Frame by Heidi Swapp

TOOLS: Fastenater by EK Success

INSTRUCTIONS

1. Lightly sand photos; mat one 5" x 7" photo on cardstock and adhere to page.

2. Add sticker to pink ghost frame. Tape one photo to back of frame and wrap with ribbons as shown. Adhere to page one.

3. Sand, mat and frame second photo; tape to page.

4. Sand and tape third photo to second page.

5. Cut two tags from white cardstock; ink edges and part of front. Use rub-ons, stickers and labels to journal and add color.

6. Use Fastenater to attach ribbons to tag with decorative staples; adhere tags to page layouts.

7. Use rub-ons to apply names onto round metal-rimmed tags. Thread with silver string and tape under photo.

8. Using foam alphabet stamps, apply both colors of acrylic paints to letters and stamp the tiles. On page one, the letters for "Paige" are cut out and matted on blue cardstock. On page two, the letters are directly stamped onto the page.

Paige and her brothers Cole, Cade, and Austin are my niece and nephews. Cole and Cade are twins and my cousins Kelly and Mike have their hands full raising them since they are all so young. They are wonderful, sweet kids, usually full of life and energy, but also very well-mannered. As you can see little Paige is wakeboarding. Cole and Cade are also already wake boarding! I think their parents have learned the secret of keeping them busy with great family activities!

145

"The Ring"

I had a dream

and it came true,
Partner
I prayed for a partner

and it was you.

Now we will be wed,

exchange rings for life
Forever
Forever we will be,

a husband and a wife.

The ring is God's idea.
Circle
A circle without end.

A constant precious reminder

that love is a gift we send.
Love
I learn to love another,

more deeply than myself.

The new life will find deepest meaning
Bible
if the Bible comes off the shelf.

For it's God who is the center

of a marriage and partner to hold,
Promises
His promises are forever,

more precious than silver or gold.

"I GIVE YOU THIS RING"

by: Dianne Frailing

APRIL 2ND

XOXO

With this R ing I thee wed...

My mom wrote "The Ring" poem for my brother Ryan and his wife-to-be, Lori. From the first time I read it I wanted to make something special with it for them to frame and display. My mom included the poem with the bridal shower favors she made for all the guests to take home. It was such a personal touch that I wanted Ryan and Lori to remember it always.

NIKKI CLEARY

Nikki is a part-time physical therapist assistant, part-time designer/teacher and full-time wife and mother. One of her aspirations is to run in a marathon, a goal she is working toward between having babies, working at her jobs and pursuing her hobbies, which include baking cakes and cookies. Her greatest love — besides her family — is designing for TweetyJill Publications and decorating her home, which she changes on a weekly basis. "I want my home to be an extension of who I am and what I love," she explains. Nikki stays busy almost every minute of the day, but happily admits that she "wouldn't change a thing." She resides in Nokomis, Florida with her husband, Sean, their child, Riley.

THE RING *Nikki Cleary*

MATERIALS

RUBBER STAMPS: Title Stamper by JustRite Stampers; Small Numbers Cube by Stampotique Originals

HYBRID INKPADS: Claret: Local Craft Store

PAPERS: Love Circle/Stripe by Pebbles, Inc.; Red Script by Scenic Route Paper Company; Girly Girl by Rusty Pickle

COMPUTER FONTS: Harrington* by Samuel Wang

WORDS, LETTERS OR STICKERS: Red/Black Chip Art Alphabet by Li'l Davis Designs

TAGS: Market Tags (Love) by Pebbles, Inc.

METAL ITEMS: Large Black Eyelets by Pebbles, Inc.; Silver Metal Ring: Local Craft Store

RIBBONS: Grandpa's Attic by SEI

ADHESIVES: Mini Glue Dots by Glue Dots International

TOOLS: Sewing Machine; Stapler; 1/8" Hole Punch; Scissors by Mundial

A curvy, Art Nouveau font available online as shareware.

INSTRUCTIONS

1. Sew papers together as shown.

2. Adhere picture and "R" with Glue Dots.

3. Type poem, leaving space to handwrite certain words you want to stand out; print out and complete poem.

4. Set eyelets in top of poem; run ribbon through eyelets and attach tags.

5. Stamp date on silver metal ring tag.

6. Staple the ribbon to the paper.

pre-Baby CLASSES

what: Boot Camp for New Dads
when: March 20, 2004
who: Sean Cleary
where: Sarasota Memorial Hospital
why: To learn how to care for a new
baby and a new mommie. (Sean
said he enjoyed it & learned quite a bit.)

what Breastfeeding Basics
when May 26, 2004
who NIKKI & SEAN CLEARY
where Sarasota Memorial Hospital
why To learn techniques & hinters. They
really encouraged spouses to come. We
both enjoyed this class & learned a lot.

what Prepared Childbirth Lamaze
when June 5th & 12, 2004
who NIKKI & SEAN CLEARY
where Sarasota Memorial Hospital
To learn breathing techniques &
ns. We also got a tour of

open

diplomas

BABIESmh
PROGRAM

BABIESmh
PROGRAM

BABIESmh
PROGRAM

PRE-BABY CLASSES
Nikki Cleary

MATERIALS

RUBBER STAMPS: Lower ABC Brush Letters by EK Success

PIGMENT INKPADS: Brown: Local Craft Store

HYBRID INKPADS: Green: Local Craft Store

PAPERS: The Paper Stack/Text Prints by DieCuts with a View

MARKERS: Size .05 Marking Pen (Black)

WORDS, LETTERS OR STICKERS: Large Funky Brush by Wordsworth; ABC's by Pebbles, Inc.

TAGS: Local Craft Store

RIBBONS: Ribbons and Rick Rack: Local Craft Store

ADHESIVES: Herma Glue Star Dotto by EK Success; Glue Dots and Glue Lines by Glue Dots International

OTHER: Baby Die Cut; Envelope; Button; String; Journaling Pockets

TOOLS: Paper Trimmer; Stapler; Scissors and Pinking Shears by Mundial

INSTRUCTIONS

1. Cut "letter" paper into a 7" x 10" rectangle and adhere with Herma Glue Star Dotto to "baby" paper.

2. Adhere ribbons to each other, then to top of page with Glue Dots and Glue Lines (do not forget to weave rick rack through the word "baby").

3. Journal on tags; ink the edges; staple ribbons to the ends and adhere tags to page.

4. Stamp "diploma" on the envelope; write the word "open" on flap and adhere envelope to page with Glue Dots.

5. Add "pre" and "classes" letter stickers to page to finish layout.

TIP

If something is too large for your page, you can always scan it into your computer and resize it to fit your space.

I wanted to remember EVERYTHING about my first pregnancy. I read every book, subscribed to weekly e-mail updates about pregnancy and took all the classes our local hospital offered us. I encouraged my husband Sean to take a "Daddy Boot Camp" class, and then we took "Lamaze" and "Breastfeeding Basics" courses together. They gave us diplomas when we completed each class. The diplomas are what inspired me to do this page, but they were too big to fit on the page. I scanned them into my computer, shrunk them down, slipped them into the envelope, and wrote all the details on the tags.

ULTRASOUND DAY
Nikki Cleary

MATERIALS

PIGMENT INKPADS: Yellow and Brown: Local Craft Store

DYE INKPADS: Brown: Local Craft Store

PAPERS: Textured Cardstock by Die-Cuts With A View; Folding Wood Tape Measures from Life's Journey by K&Company

MARKERS: Size .05 Marking Pen (Black)

WORDS, LETTERS OR STICKERS: Artic Frog; K&Company

TAGS: Local Craft Store

RIBBONS: Local Craft Store

ADHESIVES: Herma Glue Star Dotto by EK Success; Glue Dots by Glue Dots International

TOOLS: Scissors by Mundial

TIP

Scan your pictures into your computer and print them out on acid free paper so they will not fade over time.

INSTRUCTIONS

1. Tear two strips of the lighter cardstock.

2. Cut two varying widths of the tape measure paper and adhere to the top and bottom of the page. Layer and adhere torn cardstock as shown. Trim and adhere ultrasound photos to page with Herma Glue Star Dotto.

3. Journal on the tag; ink the edges with various colors, tie ribbon on and adhere to page with Glue Dots.

4. Place letter stickers on page; trace the large letters with a black pen.

As I kept growing, we kept wondering, boy or girl? We were so excited to find out! Even though we said we didn't care, Sean and I were both hoping for a boy. I remember when the ultrasound technician looked at us and asked us if we wanted to know the sex of the baby and we practically screamed "YES!" She said unmistakably, "It's a BOY," and then pointed out the proof. Tears were streaming down my face and welled up in Sean's eyes. How amazing to see the miracle the two of us created. We are truly blessed to have a healthy baby on the way.

PREGNANCY ALBUM

Nikki Cleary

MATERIALS

PAPERS: Antique Dark by Pebbles, Inc.; Card-stock, Vellum Paper: Local Craft Store

METAL ITEMS: Frame and Alphabet Charms circles by Making Memories; Metal Memorabilia Oval Frame by Li'l Davis Designs; Copper Alphabet, Frame, by K&Company

COPPER AND BLACK BRADS AND SNAPS: Local Craft Store

RIBBONS: Fibrous Ribbon: Local Craft Store

ADHESIVES: Yes! Paste by Gane Brothers & Lane Inc.; Herma Glue Star Dotto by EK Success

MESH: Copper Wire Mesh: Local Craft Store

OTHER: Album by 7gypsies

TOOLS: Pliers; Scissors by Mundial

INSTRUCTIONS

1. Cut background papers to fit album.

2. Crop pictures to desired size, back the photo with torn cardstock and some fibrous ribbon and adhere to background with copper snaps.

3. Embellish pages with metal items, letters, and copper mesh, as shown.

4. Next page place vellum on page, add fibrous ribbons, metal embellishments and frame. Tear vellum to feature photo as shown.

My mom and I were talking with my sister-in-law, Lori, about how much I wanted to have some tasteful photographs taken of me in my last trimester. Lori offered to do the photo shoot herself. I was about 38 weeks on the day we shot the photos.

P.M. to 8 P.M. Put on leotard and toe shoes. Do last minute warm-up exercises. 8 P.M. to 10:30 P.M. Performance! Take a bow!

Ballerina

Ballet
p i r o u e t t e

King Louis XIV enjoyed the dancing called "ballet" so much that he hired his dancing teacher and founded the first dancing academy in Paris 166...

*W*hen asked to describe herself, Karen uses the term "multi-tasker." She is the loving wife of husband, Jon and mother of two beautiful daughters, Lauren, five, and Sage, two and a half. She is also a full-time physician with a busy internal medicine and pediatrics practice. Scrapbooking has always been her personal form of therapy, and this year she happily opened K2 Scrapbook Studio, an avant-garde retail store that focuses on the art of scrapbooking. After living in New Orleans for more than a decade, she recently moved to Sarasota, Florida in order to be closer to her family. In describing her dedication to the craft, she says, "Some call it an obsession; I prefer to call it a commitment."

BALLERINA

Karen Hamad, M.D.

MATERIALS

PAPERS: Ballet Words (Pink) by Karen Foster Design

TRANSPARENCIES: Karen Foster Design

METAL ITEMS: Black Brads: Local Craft Store

ADHESIVES: Hermafix Tabs

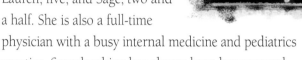

TIP

When working with transparencies, add depth to your work by placing some photos underneath the transparency and some above.

INSTRUCTIONS

1. Mount black and white photo on patterned paper.
2. Attach transparency with black brads.
3. Attach small color photo on transparency in bottom left-hand corner.

Our eldest daughter, Lauren, has a thing about ballet! Her favorite books are about Angelina Ballerina, and she has been in ballet class since the age of three. These pictures were taken backstage on the day of her second performance, and I loved the look of concentration on her face as she readied herself for the stage. I especially like the photo of her looking at herself in mirror, where I could see both her front and back in the same shot. I used the quiet colors of pastels and black and white to convey the seriousness with which she takes ballet, and let the picture and transparency do the journaling for me

TWO

Karen Hamad, M.D.

TIP

Don't be afraid to use contrasting and coordinating patterned papers. Make your selections from the same manufacturer and mix and match as you like… you can't go wrong! Remember that if you are using busy papers, a large focal point photo will have a stronger effect than many smaller ones.

MATERIALS

PAPERS: Lollipop Shoppe by Basic-Grey; Hot Pink Cardstock by Bazzill Basics; Vellum: Local Craft Store

RUB-ONS: Black Rub-Ons by Making Memories

TAGS: Lollipop Shoppe by BasicGrey

METAL ITEMS: Eyelet Phrase, Lime Green Brad and Alphabet Ribbon Charms by Making Memories

RIBBONS: Turquoise and Plaid by Doodlebug Design; Pink by Making

Memories

ADHESIVES: Hermafix Tabs; Glue Dots by Glue Dots International; Scrappy Tape by Magic Scraps

OTHER: Large Silk Flower; Small Silk Flower by Making Memories; Acrylic Flower by KI Designs

TOOLS: Hand Punch, 1 ½" Circle Punch and 2 ½" Mega Circle Punch by Marvy Uchida

INSTRUCTIONS

1. Mat photo on patterned paper of choice.

2. Cut a 7" x 12" strip of coordinating patterned paper and adhere vertically in center of pink cardstock.

3. Cut contrasting strip of 2 ½" x 9" patterned paper and mount horizontally.

4. Cut four circles out of coordinating patterned papers and position on right side. Use these circles as journaling blocks, for a title or to embellish as desired.

5. Layer large silk flower, punched circle of patterned paper, and smaller silk and acrylic flowers. Punch through all layers as necessary and attach with large brad. Use Glue Dot to adhere large flower to page.

6. Attach strips of various ribbons horizontally along left edge until they touch photo mat. Embellish with ribbon charms of choice.

My second daughter, Sage, is a source of constant amazement for me. I think I was too overwhelmed by my first child to notice most of the little things I see now as Sage grows into a toddler - the look of wonder on her face, her bold approach to new places. When we were at the park, I caught the look on her face as she was peering out of the slide at the playground that we love. Every time I look at this picture I think of where she is going to go… with me, and eventually, without me.

As you approach your second birthday, you seem fearless, inquisitive, open to all the challenges of the future...ma[...] each day bring new adventures, gre[...] loves, and bright prospects!!!

TWO

a moment in time

LBI

Karen Hamad, M.D.

TIP

Be creative in your paper tearing. Use varied papers from the same collection to create new background looks for selected pictures.

Make sure to "ground" your embellishments to page elements, i.e., attach them to photos, title blocks, journal blocks. This always looks much better than if they are free-floating on your page.

MATERIALS

FOAM STAMPS: Lowercase Script by Creative Imaginations

PAPERS: Tres Chic by American Traditional Designs

PAINTS: Banana by Making Memories

RUB-ONS: Beach by Making Memories

METAL ITEMS: Metal Embellishments by American Traditional Designs

ADHESIVES: Hermafix Tabs; Glue Dots by Glue Dots International

TOOLS: Corner Rounder Punch; Foam Brush

INSTRUCTIONS

1. Round the corners of two pictures.

2. Tear the pink and green papers in a random pattern and adhere to the background floral, showing all papers.

3. Mat bottom two pictures with polka dot paper and adhere to layout. Mat only half of photo on left.

4. Mount and "ground" (see tip) metal embellishments in corner on photos.

5. Use foam brush to cover foam stamps and stamp title.

6. Apply rub-ons to journal on bottom left corner.

Another sunny day on the beach where Lauren studiously digs for Sand Crabs!

Sometimes an outfit just screams for a specific layout and this bathing suit was made

to be scrapped on American Traditional's Tres Chic paper. I love tearing paper and

using it to create unique backgrounds for layouts.

Satisfying and simple as well!

You look fabulous

Lauren

You look fabulous

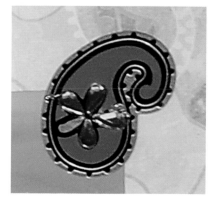

BEAUTIFUL
Karen Hamad, M.D.

MATERIALS

PAPERS: Multi Circles with Text and Pears with Script by Scenic Route Paper Company

RUB-ONS: Beach (Black) by Making Memories

METAL ITEMS: Large Decorative Staple (Fastenator) by EK Success

RIBBONS: Sheer Yellow Ribbon: Local Craft Store

ADHESIVES: Hermafix Tabs

TOOLS: Fastenator by EK Success

INSTRUCTIONS

1. Use pear paper as background; adhere a 4" x 12" border of coordinating paper on left side of page.

2. Mount photo in upper right-hand corner.

3. Cut a 2 ½" x 12" strip of contrasting paper; adhere along bottom as shown. Apply rub-ons for title.

4. Attach sheer ribbon with Fastenator at top and bottom of layout.

Mommy loves to fuss over her girls! All dressed up for her two year-old pictures, Sage is always quick to put on the "pretty princess dress" and pose for the camera! I wanted a soft but striking background with warm colors to bring out the rich velvet chair she sits on, and I used the ribbon to highlight the organza of her dress. Good thing no one can see the bubblegum stuck on the bottom of her cute Mary Janes!

GROW

Karen Hamad, M.D.

MATERIALS

PAPERS: Seed Paper by Rusty Pickle; Cardstock: Local Craft Store

METAL ITEMS: Alphadotz and Hugz by Scrapworks; Brads by American Crafts; Twill Snapz by Junkitz

RIBBONS: Local Craft Store

ADHESIVES: Hermafix Tabs; Glue Dots by Glue Dots International; Scrappy Tape by Magic Scraps

OTHER: Seed Packets; Suspender Photo

TOOLS: Xacto Knife; Stapler

INSTRUCTIONS

1. Tear seed paper; mount onto bright pink cardstock on opposite sides of two-page layout for balance.

2. Double-mat photos with contrasting cardstock and arrange them on layout.

3. Staple seed packets to cardstock, stapling around edges of packets to form journaling pocket.

4. Attach suspenders photo with metal brads; use Xacto knife to cut along side of suspender to form pocket.

5. Use Scrappy Tape to adhere ribbon along bottom of photo after clasping Twill Snapz.

6. Use soft mat to place Hugz and letters for title.

7. Staple ribbon trim to journaling tag and other to photo mats for balance.

The colors and the gardening idea fit in perfectly with Lauren's gardening class at school! I made the kids and the teacher pose in front of their prize tomatoes, and used some seed packets we had around the garage for interesting embellishments and journaling pockets. A simple title that emphasizes how quickly these kiddos "GROW" seemed to say it all!

TIP

Take pictures of subjects other than just the kids when doing a layout about one of their favorite activities. Use creative ways of hiding journaling such as making pockets from unlikely sources.

FRIENDS

Karen Hamad, M.D.

MATERIALS

RUBBER STAMPS: Artistic Lowercase Alphabet by Hero Arts

PIGMENT INKPADS: Silver or Platinum: Local Craft Store

DYE INKPADS: Medium Brown: Local Craft Store

PAPERS: Wild Asparagus by My Mind's Eye

RIBBONS: Light Green by Wild Asparagus by My Mind's Eye

FABRICS: Red and Cream Striped Fabric: Local Fabric Store

ADHESIVES: Hermafix Tabs; Glue Dots by Glue Dots International; Scrappy Tape by Magic Scraps

OTHER: Pearls; Mailbox Letter; Flowers by Prima by Martin F./Weber Co.; Buttons by Chatterbox

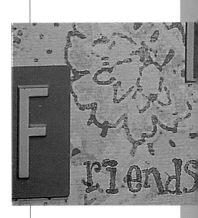

INSTRUCTIONS

1. Cut four equal squares of coordinating patterned papers. Mount on contrasting solid paper to create an interesting background, leaving small borders around each square.

2. Double-mat photo on contrasting solid papers. Mount in center of background page. Add Prima flower with pearl center to bottom right-hand corner of photo.

3. Punch three small squares; edge each square with silver ink and adhere as shown. Attach a button in each little square with a Glue Dot.

4. Use Scrappy Tape to adhere a border of green ribbon to bottom right. Tie knot and attach word charm with brad.

5. Adhere mailbox letter to bottom left for first letter of title; stamp the rest.

6. Tear fabric strip and adhere to top left with Scrappy Tape. Add three Prima flowers with pearl centers above fabric.

7. Cut journaling strips, edge with brown inkpad, and mount to page. Journal as desired.

TIP

Printing black and white photos on canvas paper - available in local photo shops - makes an interesting focal point for a beautiful and simple scrap-book layout.

This is my daughter, Lauren Renee, on the beach with her Grammy Renee (my mother) at Long Beach Island, NJ. Lauren and Grammy have always had a special bond, and spend lots of time together playing, talking and getting into mischief. We spend time every summer at our family home on the Jersey shore, a precious place for all of us. I love contrasting the generations of women in our family, and tried to create a timeless layout by printing the picture on canvas in black and white.

MORE CHEERIOS PLEASE!

Karen Hamad, M.D.

Karen Hamad, M.D.

TIP

When trying to achieve a collage effect with a title, MORE is better in terms of embellishments. Look for a variety of different mediums to work with. Use whatever doodads you can find!

MATERIALS

RUBBER STAMPS: Local Craft Store

PIGMENT INKPADS: Black: Local Craft Store

PAPERS: Cheerios by Creative Imaginations; Cardstock by Bazzill Basics

PAINTS: Asphalt and Shopping Bag by Making Memories

MARKERS: Size .05 Marking Pens (Black and Red): Local Craft Store

RUB-ONS: Scrapworks; Making Memories; Definition Monogram from Office Line by Autumn Leaves

TAGS: Metal-Rimmed Canvas by Making Memories; Leatherette Tag by Jolee's

METAL ITEMS: Heart Clip by 7gypsies; Large Eyelet by Chatterbox

RIBBONS: Black Swiss Dot: Local Craft or Fabric Store

FABRICS: Canvas Squares: Local Fabric Store

ADHESIVES: Hermafix Tabs; Glue Dots by Glue Dots International

OTHER: Stencil Letters

TOOLS: Dymo Labelmaker; Xacto knife

INSTRUCTIONS

1. Crop picture and triple-mat by layering coordinating cardstock, patterned paper and cardstock again.

2. Paint "C" stencil black and embellish with Dymo label and large brad.

3. Paint "H" stencil beige.

4. Cover "E" stencil with patterned paper; trim. Cut out stencil with Xacto knife and back with coordinating cardstock. Trim again.

5. Edge "R" with beige paint.

6. Paint half of "O" stencil beige and the other half black.

7. Attach letters unevenly to spell title and embellish with ribbon and doodads as desired.

8. Cut journal strips, edge with black paint and attach. Add journaling.

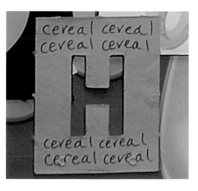

What would us mommies do without Cheerios? There are days I think that is all my kids ever eat! I wanted to make a fun layout that reflects the scattered and frazzled way I often feel at mealtime in our house… so I used the collage effect with a focus on Sage's favorite food! The picture itself wasn't that great, which is why I used a lot of bold colors and contrasting shapes to draw attention to the title and the journaling.

MARCH TO THE BEAT OF YOUR OWN DRUM

Karen Hamad, M.D.

MATERIALS

FOAM STAMPS: New Orleans by Heidi Swapp

PIGMENT INKPADS: Turquoise: Local Craft Store

PAPERS: Lollipop Shoppe by BasicGrey

PAINTS: Asphalt by Making Memories

RUB-ONS: Apple Pie by Heidi Swapp

TAGS: Lollipop Shoppe by BasicGrey

RIBBONS: Organza: Local Craft Store

ADHESIVES: Hermafix Tabs

TOOLS: Stapler

INSTRUCTIONS

1. Pick a coordinating line of papers. Tear one sheet approximately down the middle, ink the torn edges and attach by edges only to background sheet to form a pocket.

2. Punch out perforated monogram and cut title block from complementing paper, ink edges of both and adhere monogram to page.

3. Cut tags from coordinating papers.

4. Use rub-ons to complete title on title block and on smallest tag.

5. Ink edges of smallest tag and staple ribbons to top; adhere to page.

6. Ink edges of largest tag and use foam stamps and black ink to complete title.

7. Staple ribbons to tag and slip into right-hand side of pocket.

8. Cut pictures into a variety of sizes and mount on bottom of pocket.

The running joke in our family about Sage is that she really is a piece of work. Once she decides how something is going to happen, there is no convincing her otherwise! Take headbands for example… any attempt to push the band higher onto her head is met with a vehement,"No Mama, Me Do!" and she pushes it right back down onto her forehead. So I do what any self-respecting scrapbook mom would do… I grab the camera! Sage, may you always have the strength to march to the beat of your own drum!

TIP

Inking the edges of most papers and embellishments adds a whole new layer of depth to your work! Contrasts make the elements of your page "pop" and things seem less flat to the eye. Don't be afraid to get crazy with patterned paper! Most companies are creating complementing lines of various designs, so grab a handful and start tearing!

This is a collage page that I had been thinking of making for more than a year. The inspiration came from a beautiful card I found on our beloved Long Beach Island, and kept tacked up in my scrapbook area all this time! I loved cropping the tiny details out of our "not perfect" beach photos, and using them to create a montage of classic beach moments! My favorite "scraplift" to date!

BEACH DAYS
Karen Hamad, M.D.

MATERIALS

RUBBER STAMPS: Loopy Letters by Image Tree by EK Success; Mini Letters by Hero Arts

PIGMENT INKPADS: Black: Local Craft Store

DYE INKPADS: Scarlet and Turquoise: Local Craft Store

PAPERS: Wild Asparagus by My Mind's Eye; Bazzill Basics

WORDS, LETTERS OR STICKERS: Epoxy Letters (Bits and Baubles) by Creative Imaginations; Acrylic Letters by Doodlebug Design; Stickers by me and my BIG ideas

RUB-ONS: Water Rub-On by Heidi Grace

ADHESIVES: Hermafix Tabs; Glue Dots by Glue Dots International

OTHER: Seashells, Sea Glass and Star Fish by Magic Scraps; Acrylic Squares by KI Memories; Flowers by Prima by Martin F./Weber Co.

INSTRUCTIONS

1. Punch out squares and rectangles of cardstock in various colors and edge with matching color inks.

2. Punch and crop pictures in square and rectangle shapes and arrange on background paper.

3. Arrange and adhere cardstock shapes in a geometric collage pattern, leaving some blank spaces in between pieces. Embellish squares with pertinent doodads and letter stamps.

4. Journal on various larger squares.

5. Fill in gaps with stickers, rub-ons and vellum words of choice.

TIP

Using a collage format for a scrapbook page is a great way to display the pictures you have that aren't artistic enough to stand alone on a page. Have fun cropping tiny photos of crucial details, i.e., a favorite beach toy, and use as an embellishment. This is also the ideal time to use up some of those left over embellishments you've saved forever, and another way to use your alphabet stamps and inks! In a layout like this - the busier the better - a plain cardstock background is a good choice.

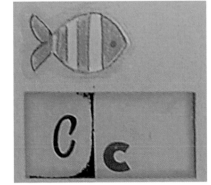
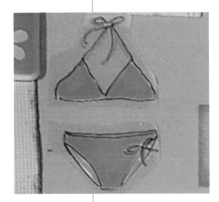

U Crack Me Up

Karen Hamad, M.D.

MATERIALS

RUBBER STAMPS: Foam Stamps by Making Memories

PAPERS: French Script by 7gypsies, Vellum by Nostalgiques by EK Success; Cardstock by Bazzill Basics

PAINTS: Asphalt by Making Memories

WORDS, LETTERS OR STICKERS: Sticko by EK Success; Creative Imaginations; The Paper Loft; Ruler Stickers and Quotes by K&Company

TAGS: Antique Ledger Tag by Nostalgiques by EK Success

METAL ITEMS: Copper "Sisters" Plaque by K&Company; Photo Anchors by 7gypsies; Brads and Eyelets by Making Memories

RIBBONS: Black Organza: Local Craft or Fabric Store

ADHESIVES: Hermafix Tabs; Glue Dots by Glue Dots International

TOOLS: Dymo Labelmaker

INSTRUCTIONS

1. Mat 5" x 7" black and white photo on black cardstock. Attach to left-hand center of background paper; add photo anchors with brads in center on either side of photo mat. Attach Dymo label to bottom left corner of photo.

2. Cut border strip of patterned vellum 3" x 12" and attach to right-hand vertical edge of background paper with eyelets.

3. Embellish antique tag with stickers and doodads of choice, add ribbon and attach to page, overlapping both border and background paper.

4. Create title with foam stamps, paint and various sticker letters.

There is something universally special about bath time in most families. It's such a comforting, familiar nightly ritual; the children are relaxed and at their best. I know I'm not the only parent that finds their little naked kids a most adorable sight, and I had fun taking these shots of my daughters as they prepared to get into the bathtub. They love to splash and horse around and are just so funny… hence, the title! I know they won't appreciate me later for having this picture published but I am thrilled to have their cute little bottoms saved for posterity (no pun intended!).

TIP

Use black and white photos and antique looking embellishments to give modern day subjects a vintage, timeless look. Also experiment with taking candid pictures of your subjects from other than the frontal perspective.

I needed a valentine for my husband Jon, and had extra wallet size photos from an early portrait taken of our baby Sage. I thought the postcard/envelope theme, with Sage as the stamp, would be perfect! I used the finished product to "send him my love!" Later I added it to Sage's album.

KISSES POSTCARD

Karen Hamad, M.D.

MATERIALS

PAPERS: Red Envelope-Printed Paper and Pink Cardstock by Club Scrap

TAGS: Jewelry Tag: Local Craft Store

METAL ITEMS: Brads, Clip, Jump Ring and Ribbon Clasp by Making Memories

RIBBONS: Red Gingham and Pink Stripe by Making Memories

ADHESIVES: Hermafix Tabs; Glue Dots by Glue Dots International; Scrappy Tape by Magic Scraps

OTHER: Buttons; Findings; Address Label; Silk Flower

TOOLS: Stapler; Decorative Stamp-Edge Scissors; Corner Rounder; Dymo Labelmaker

INSTRUCTIONS

1. Use corner rounder to round corners of mini photo. Mount on postcard.

2. Use stamp-edge decorative scissors to cut border on small photo for "stamp" in top right corner.

3. Trim red envelope-printed paper and mount to larger pink postcard paper using four pink brads in the corners. Adhere vertical strip of pink ribbon to left-hand border of "envelope."

4. Cut monogram letter with decorative stamp scissors and mount to left-hand corner with metal jump ring. Embellish with gingham ribbon run diagonally.

5. Run striped ribbon through both sides of clasp and staple ends to paper. Close clasp to create bottom border.

6. Journal on jewelry tag and clip to larger photo with mini clip.

7. Decorate envelope with flowers, findings and labels of choice.

PRODUCT RESOURCE GUIDE

100 Proof Press: www.100proofpress.com

3M / Scotch: www.scotchbrand.com

7gypsies: www.7gypsies.com

A Stamp In The Hand: www.astampinthehand.com

American Art Stamp: www.americanartstamp.com

American Crafts: www.americancrafts.com

American Tag: www.americantag.net

American Traditional Designs: www.americantraditional.com

Amy's Magic: Local Craft Store

Arctic Frog: www.arcticfrog.net

Art After Dark: 503-234-3477 (website coming soon)

ARTchix Studio: www.artchixstudio.com

Autumn Leaves: www.autumnleaves.com

BasicGrey: www.basicgrey.com

Bazzill Basics Paper: www.bazzillbasics.com

Be Unique: www.beuniqueinc.com

Beaux Regards: www.beauxregards.biz

Bo-Bunny Press: www.bobunny.com

Bravissimo! Paper: 630-833-9521

Canson: www.canson.com

Catslife Press: www.catslifepress.com

Chatterbox: www.chatterboxinc.com

Claudia Rose: www.claudiarose.com

Clearsnap, Inc.: www.clearsnap.com

Club Scrap: www.clubscrap.com

Coffee Break Designs: 317-290-1542

Collage Press: www.collagepress.com

Color Textiles: www.colortextiles.com

Colorbok: www.colorbok.com

Crafter's Pick: www.crafterspick.com

Crayola: www.crayolastore.com

Creative Imaginations: www.cigift.com

Cross-My-Heart: www.crossmyheart.com

Daisy D's Paper Co: www.daisydspaper.com

Delta: www.deltacrafts.com

Deluxe Designs: www.deluxecuts.com

DieCuts with a View: www.diecutswithaview.com

DMD Industries: www.dmdind.com

Doodlebug Design: www.doodlebug.ws/

Dritz: www.dritz.com

Dymo: www.dymo.com

Eclectic Products: www.eclecticproducts.com

EK Success: www.eksuccess.com

Embellish-It: www.embellish-it.ca/

Fibermark: www.fibermark.com

Fiskars: www.fiskars.com

FoofaLa: www.foofala.com; 1-800-588-6707

Gane Brothers & Lane, Inc.: www.ganebrothers.com

Gary M. Burlin & Company: www.garymburlin.com

Glue Dots International LLC: www.gluedots.com

Graphic Products Corporation: www.gpcpapers.com

Hampton Art: www.hamptonart.com

Heidi Grace: www.heidigrace.com

Heidi Swapp: www.heidiswapp.com

Hermafix: 1-888-CENTIS-6

Hero Arts: www.heroarts.com

Inkadinkado Rubber Stamps: www.inkadinkado.com

Jeneva & Company: www.jenevaandcompany.com

JoAnn Essentials:

Jolee's: Local Craft Store

Judi-Kins: www.judikins.com

Junkitz: www.junkitz.com

JustRite Stampers: www.justritestampers.com

K&Company: www.kandcompany.com

KI Memories: www.kimemories.com

Karen Foster Design: www.karenfosterdesign.com

KI Designs: Local Craft Store

KI Memories: www.kimemories.com

Lesley Riley: www.lalasland.com

Li'l Davis Designs: www.lildavisdesigns.com

Limited Edition Rubber Stamps: www.limitededitionrubberstamps.com

Liquitex: www.liquitex.com

Magenta: www.magentastyle.com

Magic Mesh: www.magicmesh.com

Magic Scraps: www.magicscraps.com

Making Memories: www.makingmemories.com

Marcella by Kay: Local Craft Store

Marvy Uchida: www.uchida.com

May Arts: www.mayarts.com

me & my BIG ideas: www.meandmybigideas.com

Melissa Frances: www.melissafrances.com

Memory Box: www.memoryboxscrapbooking.com

Memory Lane: www.memorylanescrapbooking.com

MOD Paper: www.loopcreations.com

Moda: www.modafabrics.com

Montreal: Local Craft Store

Mundial: www.mundialusa.com

My Mind's Eye: www.mymindseyeinc.com

Paper Adventures: www.paperadventures.com

Paper Cuts: www.papercutsthescrapbookstore.com

Paper Inspirations: www.paperinspirations.com

Paper Loft: www.paperloft.com

Paper Salon: www.papersalon.com

Paper Source: www.paper-source.com

Paperfever: www.paperfever.com

Pebbles Inc.: www.pebblesinc.com

Penny Black Rubber Stamps: www.pennyblackinc.com

Plaid Enterprises, Inc.: www.plaidonline.com

Postmodern Design: 405-321-3176

Prima by Martin/F. Weber Co.: www.weberart.com

Provo Craft: www.provocraft.com

PSX: www.psxstamps.com

Rainbow Resource Company: 707-937-0431

River City Rubberworks: www.rivercityrubberworks.com

Rubber Monger: www.rubbermonger.com

Rusty Pickle: www.rustypickle.com

Savvy Stamps: www.savvystamps.com

Scenic Route Paper Company: www.scenicroutepaper.com

Scrapworks: www.scrapworks.com

SEI: www.shopsei.com

Stampers Anonymous: www.stampersanonymous.com

Stampotique Originals: www.stampotique.com

Sticker Studio: www.stickerstudio.com

The Card Connection: Local Craft Store

The Paper Company: www.paperco.co.uk/

The Stamping Ground: www.stampingground.com

Therm O Web: www.thermoweb.com

Tombow: www.Tombow.com

Treehouse Memories: www.treehousememories.com

Two Peas in a Bucket: www.twopeasinabucket.com

United Notions: www.unitednotions.com

USArtQuest, Inc.: www.usartquest.com

Waste Not Paper: www.wastenotpaper.com

Westrim Crafts: www.westrimcrafts.com

Wordsworth: www.wordsworthstamps.com

MY FAVORITES
from page 4
by Kim Henkel

MATERIALS

DYE INKPADS: Sepia and Coffee: Local Craft Store

PAPERS: Cardstock by Doodlebug Design; Patterned Papers by DieCuts With a View; Chatterbox; Be Unique; Cross-My-Heart; MOD for Autumn Leaves; KI Memories; Melissa Frances; Doodlebug Design; Wild Asparagus by My Mind's Eye; 7gypsies; FoofaLa for Autumn Leaves; Collage Press; Basic Grey; Treehouse Memories; Anna Griffin

WORDS, LETTERS OR STICKERS: Chipboard Alphabet by Li'l Davis Designs

MARKERS: Size .05 Marking Pen (Black): Local Craft Store

TAGS: Local Craft Store

RIBBONS: Beaux Regards

ADHESIVES: Adhesive Squares by Hermafix; Glue Dots and Glue Lines by Glue Dots International

TOOLS: Sewing Machine; Aging Sponge by FoofaLa

THINGS I LOVE
from page 11
by Kim Henkel

MATERIALS

PAPERS: Cardstock by DieCuts with a View and Doodlebug Design

WORDS, LETTERS OR STICKERS: "Tags" Fabric Letters by Scrapworks; Clay Letters for "Goodies" by Li'l Davis Designs; Tall Alphabet Stickers by Chatterbox; Small Sticker Alphabet Tags by Doodlebug Design

RUB-ONS: Alphabet by Making Memories and Doodlebug Design; Flowers by KI Memories; "XXXXXXX" by 7gypsies

MARKERS: Size .05 Marking Pen (Black): Local Craft Store

TAGS: Large Purple Tag by American Tag; Floral Tag and Striped Tag by KI Memories; Mini Tags: Local Office Supply

METAL ITEMS: Eyelets and Brads by Doodlebug Design; Looped Eyelets by K&Company; Decorative Brad by Making Memories; Bulldog Clip: Local Office Supply

RIBBONS: Rick Rack by Dritz, Ribbons by KI Memories; Printed Twill by 7gypsies, Beaux Regards, Doodlebug Design and Strano Designs at Local Craft Store

FABRICS: Piece of Wool: Local Antique Store; Lace and Tulle: Local Fabric Store,

ADHESIVES: Adhesive Squares by Hermafix; Wet Glue by Magic Scraps; Decorative Floral Tape by Heidi Swapp

OTHER: Photo Corners and Chipboard Heart by Heidi Swapp; "Color" Ice Candy by KI Memories; "Memo" Note Card by 7gypsies; Safety Pin; Straight Pin; Packing String; Embroidery Floss, Piece of Old Handkerchief; Buttons; Piece of Vintage Measuring Tape

TOOLS: Sewing Machine; Embroidery Needle

STAMPS, STAMPS & MORE STAMPS
from page 12
by Kim Henkel

MATERIALS

RUBBER STAMPS: Mexican Sun by Postmodern Design; Beach Umbrella by Cherry Pie; Kewpie Doll by Hampton Art; Time Flies by Dawn Houser for Inkadinkado

RUBBER STAMPS; Artiste and Chair by Picture Show; Polka Dots, Button, Lying in Bed, Gussie Up and "I'm cold" by Stampotique Originals; Fence by 100 Proof Press; Studio by The Stamping Ground; Madame Paris and Ink Bottles by A Stamp in the Hand; Queen Bee by Catslife Press; Eiffel Tower, Sweet and Ooh La La by Paper Salon, XOXO Heart by Paper Inspirations; Tiny Prints by Hero Arts; House by Magenta; Stars in Square by Art After Dark; Alphabet Stamps by Stampotique Originals, Hampton Art, AB Seas, Postmodern Design and JustRite Stampers; Heart in Hand: Local Craft Store

DYE INKPADS: Sepia, Coffee, Orange, Pink, Greens, Reds, Burgundy, Yellow, Brown and Black: Local Craft Store

HYBRID INKPADS: Rainbow: Local Craft Store

PAPERS: Cardstock by Doodlebug Design and Bazzill Basics

TAGS: Local Craft Store

RIBBONS: Local Craft Store

ADHESIVES: Adhesive Squares by Hermafix

OTHER: Mini Coin Envelope by Waste Not Paper

TOOLS: Pinking Shears by Mundial; Aging Sponge by FoofaLa